THE STORY OF YOU ONLY LIVE TWICE

Fleming, Bond and Connery in Japan

Graham Thomas

This text-only edition has been formatted for Kindle using Kindle Create so that readers are able to resize the text to suit their reading needs.

This is also the format for paperback.

A full colour mightily illustrated version is also available on Amazon. This maintains the look of the original edition but it does not allow the reader to resize the text and is therefore unsuitable for smaller screens such as phones but works well with tablets.

© Graham Thomas 2018. Third edition for Kindle and paperback. First and Second Edition published 2015 on iBooks. This edition updated May 2019.

ISBN: 978-1-911489-95-5

The right of Graham Thomas to be identified as the author of the work has been asserted herein in accordance with the Copyright, Designs and Patents Act,1988.

All rights reserved. This book is distributed subject to the condition that it shall not, by way of trade or otherwise, be lent, resold, reworked, hired out or otherwise circulated without the publishers prior and written consent in any form of binding, cover or e-version, pdf or any other electronic version other than that in which it is published and without a similar condition including this condition being imposed on the subsequent purchaser.

Unless otherwise stated all images are the authors. When any James Bond, Ian Fleming, book or film creative assets are featured or referred to they remain the copyright of the holders. The James Bond novels are the property of Ian Fleming Publications Ltd, and Danjaq, LLC and United Artists Corporation are usually the trademark and copyright holders of all things film. Also note that this book is not an official book linked to these entities.

Sources can be found in the Bibliography. Every effort has been made by the author and publisher to ensure that copyright is properly identified. Any mistakes are unintentional and the legal copyright owner should make contact and the error will be acknowledged and rectified. (See end of book for contact details.)

This book has been legally deposited with the British Library.

CONTENTS

FOREWORD	1
HERBERT O YARDLEY AND THE COLOUR PURPLE	7
HONG KONG	16
ALCOHOLICS SYNONYMOUS	23
TOKYO	29
SOMERSET MAUGHAM	40
TOKYO 1962	43
FLEMING VISITS JAPAN, 1962	47
RICHARD HUGHES	68
TORAO SAITO	77
XAVIER KOIKE	85
BOND	86
SHATTERHAND	105
THE CIA's ASSESSMENT	107
THE FOOD	109
PRODUCTION STARTS	115
CONNERY ON LOCATION	125
THE FILM	141
THE MAN WITH THE RED TATTOO	149
POSTSCRIPT	157
THE AUTHOR	162

BIBLIOGRAPHY

FOREWORD

You Only *Live Twice* was the final Bond novel published during Fleming's lifetime, landing in book stores on 16 March 1964. It was the twelfth in the series but the first to use the Far East, and specifically Japan, as a setting. Two years later it became the fifth film. This Japanese setting was an unusual departure as most of the Bond novels (and the first four films) were firmly rooted in Europe, the US, and the Caribbean.

Interestingly, although Fleming had a narrow horizon when it came to Bond's travels, he had not entirely ignored the Far East in earlier novels. In 1959 when writing the Bond short stories collected under the title *Quantum of Solace*, he has Bond remarking while attending a party and contemplating marriage, 'if I don't find an air hostess there'll be nothing for it but to marry a Japanese...'

In 1957 when writing *Dr No*, both the Eurasian wicked doctor and Bond wear *kimono* - although Bond feels he looks idiotic in it.

Even earlier in 1955, in *Diamonds Are Forever*, Bond remarks on the subject of marriage (again), that if he were to marry, it wouldn't last as he'd suffer claustrophobia, he'd leave and 'get myself sent to Japan or somewhere.'

In *Moonraker* written in 1954 we read in Chapter 8 that Bond consults a file called 'Philopon. A Japanese murder-drug.'

'Philopon is the chief factor in the increase in crime in Japan.

According to the Welfare Ministry there are now 1,500,000 addicts in the country, of whom one million are under the age of 20, and the Tokyo Metropolitan Police attribute 70 per cent of juvenile crime to the influences of the drug.'

Philopon was a methamphetamine used by the Japanese military; Fleming then refers to the Bar Mecca murder case, which is said to have been a real life case. Mecca was a bar in Tokyo and, in 1953, a businessman was murdered in an upstairs room which was usually used by musicians as their rest room. The illegal distribution of Philopon was said to be the root cause for the crime.

But going back to the very first book, *Casino Royale*, how did Bond gain his 007 designation? By killing a Japanese cypher expert who was working on cracking British codes in New York. And when Le Chiffre is torturing him, he recalls that colleagues who had been tortured by the Germans and Japanese told him that towards the end, the victim could be overcome by a feeling of sexual languor where pain becomes pleasurable.

As will become apparent over the course of this book, these earlier references are possibly more than prescient when Fleming came to write *You Only Live Twice* in 1963.

My personal interest in Japan sparked the idea of putting this book together, although I took a rather tortuous route to bring it to fruition. When young, I had watched all the early Bond films in the cinema up to the first one or two Roger Moore films before I grew out of them. *You Only Live Twice* was a favourite and was one reason - albeit of a number - that my my interest in Japan was lit.

Looking back, it now seems somewhat bizarre that I first saw the film when camping on the island of Guernsey. The Odeon was the single cinema in St Peter Port, and when the Germans occupied the island during the Second World War they took it over and played only German language films..

As an adolescent I had read all the books, which I had borrowed from the library. Many years later I moved to Japan where a number of separate strands of interest began to intertwine, all of which led ultimately to this book. For example, I started to collect volumes of *This is Japan* long before I realised that the editor had been a friend of Ian Fleming and a character in the novel. It was also through these volumes that I discovered that Fleming had visited Japan not once but twice, and that potentially an interesting story was there to be uncovered.

Back in the mid 1990s, I stayed at the New Otani Hotel and it was a concierge who asked the question, did I know that it had been a location for *You Only Live Twice*? No, I replied.

And then I moved to Japan. By this time, the embryonic web was becoming established and this enabled me to start undertaking some early research. I also had a laser disc copy of the film that offered higher resolution than a video tape. One of the first things I found was that almost nothing new had been published about Fleming and his Japan connections, and already misinformation had been published about where the film had been shot in Japan.

I ought to add here that by no means am I being critical of the many people who have undertaken their own quest but if you live in a country, and know the country well, there is by default a greater chance that you can be more accurate. The second reason that perhaps I can write more comprehensively now than those early pioneers is that while many of the people associated with the novel and film are dead, there is now a lot more that is accessible online or can be more readily tracked down and purchased. None of this is being boastful and undoubtedly I have made my own errors that will be gleefully pointed out.

Initially I started on a quest to identify the real film locations and these I started to publish on a web page in the early 2000s. Of more interest was the quest to find out more about Fleming's visits and not just Fleming but the travels of Bond across Japan as laid out in the novel.

Before writing the novel, Fleming had made two trips to Japan. His first took place when writing a series of articles about the world's most 'thrilling cities.' A few years later he returned to research Japan's culture specifically for *You Only Live Twice* which, for many of its pages, is a diary of Bond's travels from Tokyo to the island of Kyushu mimicking the same journey that Fleming undertook.

When this was turned into a film, the Japanese setting was retained, and Connery and the film crew arrived in Japan to shoot on location - but more on this later.

For those whose knowledge of Fleming is scanty, a quick recap. Ian Lancaster Fleming was born in London on 28 May 1908, the second of four brothers. The family had Huguenot and Scottish ancestors and, due to the business dealings of his paternal grandfather, the family became well-off, Fleming was educated at Eton, and then abroad at universities in Germany and Switzerland.

Having failed to secure a place in the Foreign Office, his writing career began tentatively at the Reuters news agency. He was later to say that this was a good place to train as they insisted on a simple straightforward writing style, and an emphasis on getting the facts right. However he resigned in 1933 when offered the lucrative chance of becoming a banker and then a stockbroker. Unfortunately Fleming was largely an unsuccessful one, failed to make his fortune but remained in the job until 1939.

In 1933, his elder brother Peter, had visited the Far East as Special Correspondent for *The Times*, principally to China and Manchuria but also he made a brief visit to Japan. (He also wrote an article for the *Listener* on Manchuria.) Subsequently, he said that his stay in Tokyo was not long for him to make any comment of interest about the capital. He returned in 1935 when he met the diplomat Sir George Samson who's wife wrote, 'We have just had a delightful few days with the young man Peter Fleming as our guest, a remarkable young man.'

At the outbreak of World War 2, Ian Fleming was commissioned in the Royal Naval Reserve and began working as an assistant to the Director of Naval Intelligence in the Admiralty, London. Over the war years he increasingly became involved with clandestine adventures, spies and commando missions. These experiences became the genesis of the Bond books and characters.

Following the war he decided to return to the world of journalism and was appointed foreign manager in charge of overseas correspondents for Kemsley, then owners of the *Sunday Times* (which at the time was independent of *The Times*) and other papers. He accepted their offer on condition that he could have two months holiday every year. The salary was also a handsome £4,500.

It was not until 1952 that he wrote the first of the Bond novels. *Casino Royale* was written in less than three months, sold to the publisher Jonathan Cape, reviews were positive and a cultural icon was born. He published a further fourteen James Bond titles, each one growing in success. Almost all were written in his Jamaica home, Goldeneye.

Despite this soaring success Fleming continued with his day job into the very early 1960s. In part this was because he worried constantly about money, and was unconvinced that he could sustain the popularity of the novels. In part it was a job that also helped him with the books: he could ask foreign correspondents for local details that would then be incorporated within the plots, and his job allowed him to travel too, which is how he came to Japan for the first time. Nevertheless, even after leaving, he was kept on a retainer of £1,000 per annum. Now his own man, Fleming was able to make a return trip to Japan in order to get the factual details correct for his planned novel.

This return trip was recorded by his travel companion Richard Hughes and became one of the three core sources for starting my research - the others being the chapter on Tokyo that Fleming wrote for the book *Thrilling Cities*, and *You Only Live Twice* itself. All three provide a firm foundation but none are perfect when it comes to the detail as they often leave gaps and, indeed, have their own inconsistencies and errors. These needed to be filled and corrected respectively.

A first edition was published in 2015. For the second edition I added two further chapters: on food and the follow-on novel

Graham Thomas

The Red Tattoo, as well as adding images, and more information where this has become more recently available. (I wonder sometimes if there will be ever a time when nothing further can be found.) For the illustrated Kindle edition, more images have been added as well as some additional detail.

But before diving into the story, first a little piece of fairly unknown background about a spy who might well have had some minor influence when Fleming was writing *You Only Live Twice*.

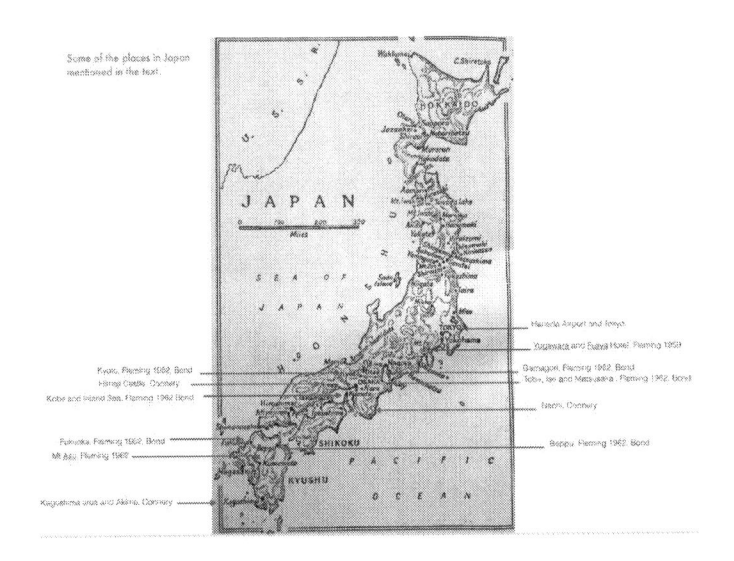

HERBERT O YARDLEY AND THE COLOUR PURPLE

In early 1959, Ian Fleming contributed a three-page preface to a book on how to win at poker: *The Education of a Poker Player* was a best seller written by Major Herbert O. Yardley. It turned out to be a book that had some influence on Fleming's subsequent writing.

Born in Indiana in 1889 according to Yardley but 1881 according to the CIA, Major Yardley was one of America's most (self-titled) brilliant cryptographers, working for the US government in pre-CIA days during the First World War and then through the 1920s. He established the first code-breaking agency in the US but due to funding cuts and a change of government policy, the bureau he launched closed, leaving him angry, frustrated and without a job. In 1930 a disaffected Yardley wrote *The American Black Chamber*, a book that exposed many of the secrets of what he and his colleagues had done. Result? A best seller, fame, and some fortune but he was ostracised by most of his colleagues, his former employers, and the spying Establishment generally.

One of his most startling revelations was that the US had been cracking Japanese coded intelligence since 1920 - albeit just one of 21 countries that they were spying on - and this had left Japan in a significantly disadvantaged position when it came to agreeing an international treaty at the Limitation of Armaments Conference of 1921-22. Indeed they had intercepted and decoded a message from the Japanese government to Admiral Baron Kato who was at the Conference that showed what Japan was prepared to concede.

The use of this intelligence by the US led to a negotiated reduction in Japan's naval strength, and once they learnt that they had been duped, the Japanese were understandably livid. One consequence - one that had long-term global repercussions - was that this led to a shift in the responsibilities for foreign policy from Japan's Foreign Office to the military.

Not surprisingly Yardley's book became a sensation in Japan after it was translated and published in 1931. The *Burakku Chiyemba*, as it was called, sold by the thousands, and two major newspapers, the *Osaka Mainichi* and the *Tokyo Nichi-Nichi*, serialised the book, along with interviews with Yardley.

The Japanese press were outraged by the US's treachery and they stoked anti-West sentiment with headlines such as 'Betrayal of International Trust,' 'Treachery at the Washington Conference,' 'Disgrace to the Convener of the Conference.' Two American pilots who had flown into Japan without advanced notice were detained for a number of weeks on suspicion of spying. Of course it also led to the Japanese significantly and quickly upgrading their security and codes: before the revelation they had created codes manually but now they built a cypher-machine that became their principle source of codes across the 1930s and into the 1940s. The first model was called Red before it was upgraded to Purple.

In the meantime Yardley spent all the money he had made from *The American Black Chamber* on a rather lavish, sometimes exciting, sometimes disastrous lifestyle; he went into a number of business ventures that failed; he wrote some reasonably successful spy novels including *Red Sun of Nippon*. This featured a young American State Department officer who falls in love with a beautiful Chinese-American girl who then helps him uncover Japan's preparation for the invasion of Manchuria.

He spent a largely unhappy and unsuccessful time as a Hollywood scriptwriter although one of his roles was advising on the film *Rendezvous* that was a film version of his novel *The Blonde Countess*.

Then at the end of the 1930s, he spent a short time working in China where he was able to crack the Japanese Army's field codes and cyphers. His presence did not go unnoticed by the Japanese government who dispatched a message to its embassies warning that 'the Chungking Government has '...made the American, Yardley, an adviser....'

According to the message Yardley had employed 700 to 800 people to crack the codes and it was thought they were doing this successfully so the embassies were asked to be vigilant and to ensure they locked their safes at night in case treacherous agents were at work within the building. However, all evidence points to Yardley and his team continuing to gather some significant intelligence despite whatever precautions the Japanese took.

At the end of his contract, he was taken on by the Canadian intelligence service but following pressure from both the US and UK governments his employment was curtailed.

At this point there is a possible intersection with Fleming who had come to the US in 1941 to foster collaborative relationships between US and British intelligence. William Stephenson headed up the British operation and it is claimed that on the visit, to demonstrate their capabilities, Stephenson set up an operation to steal codes from the Japanese Consulate in New York, with Fleming as part of the team. By pure chance, the

Consulate was on the floor below Stephenson's offices in the Rockefeller Centre. Stephenson had discovered that coded messages were being sent from here to Tokyo and decided that the nature of these should be determined. The team broke into the Consulate, removed the codebooks, copied them, and then returned them without, apparently, the Japanese ever being the wiser.

Fleming in part was able to persuade the Americans to provide the British with two replicas of their Japanese cipher machines so they could obtain their own MAGIC decrypts - and this will be explained in more depth later in the chapter. And ironically when it comes to the fractured relationship between the US and British Intelligence that forms the fulcrum for the plot in *You Only Live Twice*, Fleming advised the Americans on how they could improve the organisational efficiency of their intelligence operation.

Back to Yardley. By the middle of the 1940s, Yardley was largely pursuing his preferred life of leisure *aka* wine, women and song funded by his success at poker playing.

He had first sat around a card table in the saloons and bars of Worthington, Indiana when he was sixteen, and because of his flair for maths and his photographic memory, he soon found that he could win consistently. Over the years, he refined his technique and understanding not only of the game but also most importantly of the players, and eventually he realised that he could make good money by penning a book on how to win at the tables.

The Education of a Poker Player was published in the US in 1957 and quickly sold over 100,000 copies not least because it not only covered the techniques of poker playing but also spun ripping yarns of games, espionage, and other stories about the author's life and travels.

Fleming bought a copy after a friend alerted him to its publication in the US, and was so impressed that he urged his publisher, Jonathan Cape, to reissue the book in Britain. Cape only agreed on condition that he wrote a preface, realising that the attachment of Fleming's name would likely guarantee sales.

Fleming opened his preface with his disdain for what he considered to be the hypocritical laws on gambling in the UK.

'If it were possible to have worse laws than our sex laws they would be the laws that regulate gambling... To deal only with what is relevant to this brief note, while twenty million adults gamble on the football pools each week, ten million on horse-racing and five million on premium bonds, playing poker for money, a legal game over half the world including most of the British Commonwealth, is illegal.'

In fact almost one third of the preface is taken up with this criticism before he moves on to explain why he admires the book, a combination of the brilliant instruction about playing poker and 'some of the finest gambling stories I have ever read,' before he finishes by describing how poor he himself was as a poker player.

By the time the book appeared in 1959, Yardley was dead, and he and Fleming had, so far as is known, never met. (His grave can be found close to that of J F Kennedy in Arlington Cemetery.)

If he wasn't a traitor, Yardley was certainly a whistle-blower so it is interesting that Fleming as part of the British spying establishment was prepared to support Yardley's book. Of course it may have been no more than hard commerce: Fleming could see that the book would add further credence to the Bond but more importantly Fleming myth - even though neither were great poker players themselves. Perhaps he rather admired the rakish life that Yardley had lived; we certainly know that Fleming was becoming increasingly distanced from the UK's spying professionals who he thought had not kept alive the traditions of the Service. And he had no love of the Americans. So here was a way that he could be a minor irritation by cocking-a-snoop at the intelligence establishment.

Having written his preface for Yardley's book, Fleming then wrote an article for *The Spectator*. Published in October 1959, it was titled 'If I were Prime Minister' and laid out Fleming's manifesto for a radical reform of the United Kingdom, which included reforming the laws relating to sex and gambling. Clearly he was on a crusade:

'Next I should proceed to a complete reform of our sex and gambling laws and endeavour to cleanse the country of the hypocrisy with which we so unattractively clothe our vices...' He wrote that he would turn...'the Isle of Wight into one vast pleasure dome (cf. Fr. Baisodrome) which would be a mixture of Monte Carlo, Las Vegas, pre-war Paris and Macao...This would be a world where the frustrated citizen of every class could give full rein to those basic instincts for sex and gambling which have been crushed through the ages. At last our cliff-girt libido would have an outlet and the sleazy strip-tease joints, rump-sprung street-walkers and backroom card games would be out of business forever...'

So did Yardley's book influence Fleming in any other ways?

It seems possible that with its stories of a licentious life of gambling and prostitution in Hong Kong and China it acted as one (but probably not the only) impetus for the places Fleming would visit when, a short time later, he wrote his series of articles for the *Sunday Times* about the world's thrilling cities. This series included two featuring Hong Kong and neighbouring - and very seedy - Macau.

Yardley had come to Hong Kong when the Chinese employed him. He arrived to be met by his interpreter Ling Fab who had been instructed to provide everything for Yardley's comfort. Largely, this meant cocktails and women.

The descriptions of the spies, journalists, crooks, dubious and slimy expats, and not least the prostitutes in the Chinese city of Chungking perhaps had indeed acted as some stimulus for Fleming to visit the Far East - though Yardley was by no means the first to write of such intrigue, and it is also clear that Fleming was familiar with *The World of Suzie Wong*, a book that definitely provides a backdrop for his visit to Hong Kong.

However it seems possible that the book influenced at least one minor similarity: at the same time as he was reading Yardley's book, Fleming was writing *For Your Eyes Only*. Yardley writes, 'It is said sooner or later everyone of any note comes to the Cafe de la Paix in Paris to sip a drink and watch the crowd.' In *For Your Eyes Only* Fleming writes that Bond regularly took lunch at the Cafe de la Paix, where 'the food was good enough...and it amused him to watch the people.'

In *You Only Live Twice* there is certainly some cross-over between Yardley's world and Fleming's, which I summarise here but will refer to again in later chapters.

At the start of the novel, Bond is in M's bad books having fallen into an alcoholic fuelled depression following the murder of his wife Tracy Bond. Given one final chance to redeem himself, Bond is dispatched on a mission is to negotiate with the Japanese secret service for access to their intelligence on the Russians. Fleming writes that since the War, the Japanese have been building state-of-the-art decoding machines to crack the most secret of Russian messages. However, for various political reasons, while they had been passing on this intelligence to the CIA, they had not been passing it to the British; nor was the CIA then passing it on to the British other than in a redacted summary.

Graham Thomas

Bond arrives in Tokyo to negotiate a swop: Japan's intelligence for British high-grade intelligence on China that was coming from their network within the country codenamed the Macau Blue Route.

Fleming called the Japanese cryptography machine MAGIC 44. In real life MAGIC was the name given to the US cryptography team that was responsible for cracking Japanese codes during World War 2. Fleming refers to the Macau Blue Route: in real life the Japanese had their Red, Blue and Purple coding machines.

M, when explaining the mission to Bond, says that a couple of top CIA cryptographers had defected to the Soviet Union and here Fleming may have been carefully hinting at Yardley being a defector or at least a traitor. But was he?

It was only some years later in 1967 that a dramatic claim was made: yes Herbert Yardley was a traitor! Yardley had sold secrets to the Japanese back in the late 1920s. In other words he was a man who would work for anyone, at any time, perhaps even at the same time. More than a double-agent perhaps even a triple agent.

In *The Broken Seal,* the espionage writer Ladislas Farago claimed that during the summer of 1928 Yardley sold the secrets of his cryptology work to the Japanese for the sum of $7,000. Farago's account laid out that Yardley had met with Setsuzo Sawada, an official in the Japanese Embassy when Yardley offered to hand over decrypted Japanese diplomatic messages. In addition, he would explain how these had been decrypted, and how the US were creating their own cypher systems.

Farago's claim was met with much incredulity among many former spies. Their view was that while the rogue Yardley had been wrong in publishing his books, he was no traitor, and that any evidence to the contrary was a face-saving fabrication by the

Japanese government in the light of Yardley's original story on how he had decoded their intelligence.

However since then more evidence has emerged that points to Yardley having colluded with the Japanese and that off-and-on he might have been doing this until the attack on Pearl Harbour. Not only that but it was very likely the US government were more than aware of his actions. Was he in fact a double agent? And although the Americans had the cryptologists it would seem almost foolhardy not to call on Yardley's skills during the course of the Second World War. So perhaps he used his poker playing as a cover.

Fascinating stuff. Fascinating because if true, does that not explain why he was buried in Arlington? Surely not the place where a traitor would be interred.

Perhaps Fleming did possess inside knowledge about Yardley that was woven into *You Only Live Twice* but we will now never know. What we do know is that the genesis of the novel started with a trip that Fleming made to the Far East in 1959.

HONG KONG

The chapters in Fleming's book *Thrilling Cities* first appeared individually as so-called 'mood pieces' in the UK's *Sunday Times*. These were thirteen essays written between 1959 and 1960 by Fleming - who was still a manager on the newspaper despite having published seven Bond novels.

Of the cities visited, seven he named as world cities and six as European; they included Hong Kong, Macao, Tokyo, Los Angeles, Berlin and Vienna. Each was written by Fleming to focus on, as he described it, the bizarre and shadier side of life. They of course played on his fame as the writer of the Bond novels, and his brief from the editor had been to include exotic aspects of the cities that Bond himself would enjoy - although when they came to be published in the newspaper they were censured versions of Fleming's prose as it was felt that some aspects of Fleming's exploration might upset the *Sunday Times*' reader. (It was only when *Thrilling Cities* was published in 1963 by Jonathan Cape that these passages appeared for the first time.)

'He writes about them brilliantly, impressionistically, as no one else would...' gushed the publisher's publicity. In the forward to the book, Fleming writes that he had always been interested in adventure and when visiting places overseas had enjoyed the frisson of leaving wide, well lit streets and venturing into the back alleys.

The Definitive Story Of You Only Live Twice

In March 1959, *Goldfinger* had appeared in book stores and despite some so-so reviews raced to the top of the best seller lists. This should have been a moment of celebration but by now Fleming's health was beginning to wither and he suffered reoccurring problems with his heart, kidneys and back, not least because of smoking 60 cigarettes a day and drinking significant quantities of alcohol. On top of this, his marriage remained fraught. So perhaps when Fleming left London on a November morning in 1959 with £500 of travellers' cheques in his wallet, he looked forward to a degree of freedom and, as his features editor Leonard Russell had remarked before he left, a trip that might provide him with more useful background material for his Bond books. Not that this in fact was something new. James Bond was rooted in Fleming's own - albeit exaggerated - experiences, and he needed to continue to seek these out to feed the books. This had always been the case. Back in 1953, shortly after the publication of *Casino Royale*, he had been sent out on assignments for the *Sunday Times* that would subsequently be further developed and appear in the early novels.

Fleming's round-the-world ticket cost £803 19s and 2d. At this time aircraft flew with no classes other than one that today would be designated First Class. With his ticket in hand, and a visa in his passport (in those days a visa had to be obtained from the Japanese London Embassy before travel), he checked-in at the BOAC's terminal building in the centre of London before being taken on a rather dank morning to board a BOAC Comet 4 G/ADOK (although either he or the printer made a mistake with the aircraft registration as BOAC Comets all had registrations beginning with AP -). Flying from London Airport the Comet stopped *en-route* at various places as in those days flying non-stop was impossible. These stops included Beirut (described as 'the great smuggling junction of the world'), mud-coloured Bahrein, which he thought was the scruffiest airport in the world, and New Delhi, before finally drifting down to Hong Kong's

Kai Tak airport, arriving in the early morning some twenty-six hours after leaving London.

(In fact, the Comet had only first started flying this route some months earlier, and to celebrate, BOAC had printed their own 'first day' stamp cover.)

For reading matter, Fleming had brought a proof copy of Eric Ambler's *Passage of Arms* as in the Golden Age of Travel there were no inflight magazines nor inflight entertainment – other than seven course meals, limitless alcohol, and no rules regarding smoking including pipes and cigars. Fleming, though, was one of those people who enjoyed air travel and who was excited about arriving in a new city. No doubt too, he was treated like royalty on the flight.

Hong Kong was a booming but densely crowded city in 1959. During the preceding decade Chinese migrants had poured over the border and while many of the squalid shantytowns had been torn down, the apartment blocks that had replaced them were densely built. The most notorious district was the Kowloon Walled City, a largely Triad infested and ungovernable area of 2 hectares with tens of thousands of residents. Fleming however was not staying here nor in a hotel but with Hugh and Rose Marie Barton, two close friends of his brother Peter. After Sir Robert 'Robin' Brown Black, the Territories' Governor, Hugh Barton was one of the most powerful men in the territory as he headed up Jardine, the omnipresent trading company, and was a director of umpteen other organisations as well as having a seat on the colony's Executive Council. Rose Marie was the daughter of the industrialist Vilhelm Meyer who had been a driving force behind the modernisation of industrial China in the first part of the twentieth century, and the two had met and married in Shanghai.

The Bartons (along with their daughter Susannah when she was not attending school in the UK) lived in a villa on the slopes of Shek-O above Big Wave Bay in the south east corner of Hong Kong Island. [A little bit of geography: Hong Kong was then and still is made of three distinct territories: Kowloon and the New Territories known by Old China Hands as the mainland as it is part of the China landmass; Hong Kong Island a short ferry ride from Kowloon is the seat of Government, the commercial centre, and where most of the ex-pats live; and thirdly the myriad of smaller islands scattered around the South China Sea.]

In the 1950s, most well-off ex-pats usually lived high on The Peak where the temperatures would be cooler, and so the Bartons were unusual in having a house that was in the south of the island. On the other hand, Big Wave Bay is one of the island's prettiest and most accessible beaches, and Shek-o itself was a small traditional fishing village. It would have offered a haven of tranquility away from the bustle and noise of the city, and perhaps this is why the Bartons decided to live there.

It is clear that Fleming fell in love with Hong Kong immediately, 'the most vivid and exciting city I have ever seen' is how he described it, going on to say, 'he would recommend it without reserve to anyone who possesses the fare.' He cited the countryside, golf, horse racing, restaurants, and the cheap but excellent tailoring as all good reasons to come.

During his short stay in Hong Kong, his companion in crime was not Hugh Barton - who was far too well mannered to be pounding the streets where Suzie Wong could be found - but journalist Richard Hughes. (And much can be read about the formidable Mr Hughes in a later chapter.) On hitting the streets of Hong Kong Island, Fleming was immediately struck by the cacophony of neon light.

They kicked-off their evening in a bar run by an ex- Shanghai policeman called Jack Conder. This could be found 22A Queens Road Central and it was here that Fleming became an honourary member of Alcoholics Synonymous. (A subject that warrants its own chapter.) Once inducted and lubricated, Fleming and Hughes went on to Wanchai. Their destination was the Peking Restaurant at 20-24 Lockhart Rd. Having opened in the 1950s it had quickly become an institution: a *gweilo* friendly establishment that served northern Chinese food in a way that suited the less than adventurous taste buds of the expat.

While Peking Duck was the house dish the sizzling prawns and the minced pigeon with lettuce were also to be recommended. In the end, Fleming wrote that he ate, 'Shark's fin soup with crab, shrimp balls in oil, bamboo shoots with seaweed, chicken and walnuts, with, as a main dish, roast Peking duckling, washed down with mulled wine. Lotus seeds in syrup added a final gracious touch.'

However, it was unlikely that he was drinking mulled wine but rather *huangjiu* a Chinese alcoholic beverage that comes in many forms but can be dark, sweet and drunk warm.

Among the things that Richard Hughes brought up in conversation was the grave lack of hotels, something that Hugh Barton would help to alleviate within a few years when he led the plan to build the Mandarin Oriental in Central. Hughes also confided that Japanese mistresses were better than Chinese - an irony as he would marry many years later Oiying (Ann) Lee, the daughter of a Chinese general who had served in Chiang Kai-shek's Nationalist army. (But by then he had probably forgotten this conversation.) He confided too that the latest scandal in Hong Kong was the proliferation of massage parlours and the blue cinemas (with colour and sound!) that flourished in Kowloon. Prostitutes could be found roaming the aisles of these cinemas offering their services before (and most definitely after) porn films were shown. Live sex shows were common and it was said that they were filmed before being re-shown on the big screen.

Hughes or more likely Fleming might have been exaggerating that this was a scandal: prostitution has always been legal in

Hong Kong, only the way it is carried out is controlled, and blue films were never banned, indeed no film had a classification so any films could be projected. So the world of Suzie Wong that they visited next was indeed a real world even if Miss Wong herself was something of a myth.

Fleming was an admirer both of Richard Mason's novel, *The World of Suzie Wong*, and *A Many Splendoured Thing* by Han Suyin. He appeared to be attracted to the idea of a Western man falling in love with a Chinese or Eurasian girl possibly because he thought it was, as he described it, 'an unpopular topic with the great union of British womanhood.' This accorded with Fleming's view of British women who he said never washed, had no idea of how to make love properly, and were either prudish or mercenary.

In order to get a sense of the myth first hand, Fleming and Hughes paid a visit to the Luk Kwok Hotel, renamed in Mason's book as the Nam Kok House of Pleasure. Mason had stayed in the hotel when writing the novel, building the story around the painter Robert Lomax who befriended and, after much misadventure, finally marries the prostitute Suzie Wong.

Fleming found the Luk Kwok Hotel thriving. 'Solitary girls may still not sit unaccompanied in the spacious bar with its great and many-splendoured juke-box. You must still bring them in from outside, as did Lomax, to prevent the hotel becoming, legally, a disorderly house.' Fleming was asked whether he would like to meet a friend of Suzie's, as Suzie herself was now a recluse but he turned down the offer, and returned to the comfort of the Barton's villa for the night.

The next day would be spent in the Portuguese territory of Macau before both men flew on to Tokyo.

Some years later Fleming was interviewed for *Tatler* magazine when he remarked that the city he had found to be the most exciting was Hong Kong.

'It's just enough to eat the delicious Chinese food, see beautiful girls wearing *cheong sams*. Maybe it is beautiful in a squalid kind of way but even the smell of cheap frying oil and bean curd is exciting in that context. I know all about the poverty and the refugee problem but what is so staggering and so delightful is that everybody looks so happy, clean, dignified. Then all the junks and the battleships in the Bay, so splendid. Hong Kong is also one of the few places where they understand the use and subtlety of neon lighting...violets, and crimsons and blues...'

ALCOHOLICS SYNONYMOUS

Who else could have co-founded Alcoholics Synonymous after moving from Tokyo to Hong Kong? Richard Hughes of course. And wasn't it natural that Hughes should invite Fleming to a special gathering of the Alcoholics to celebrate the fourth anniversary of its founding.

Alcoholics Synonymous had been the brainchild of Hughes and the aforementioned Jack Conder – who proved to be almost the equal of Hughes when it came to Hong Kong legends, and was certainly the type of character that Fleming warmed to naturally. (And a brief digression here might be of interest.)

One of thirteen kids, Conder had left home in the north east of England when his mother was widowed in 1924. He joined the Royal Army Medical Corp and was posted to Shanghai in 1927, sailing on the *Kildonan Castle* from Tilbury to Hong Kong in 28 days. Here he was billeted at the Peninsula Hotel – then still in the final stages of construction - before taking an old P&O tub named *Kammala* to Shanghai - along with various other battalions, all of who were acting as guards around the perimeter of the International Settlement. In 1928, having completed his Army Service, Conder joined another 400 ex-pats in the Shanghai Police. Their main duty was to crack down on the opium trade, which along with gambling and prostitution was the way the gangs made money.

When not pursuing the gangs (and in particular the Green Gang), Conder could often be found in the rather more gentile surroundings of the Astor House Hotel's tea dances, a popular pastime for ex-pats, where he taught foreign and Chinese girls to dance foxtrots and waltzes. It was here he met his future wife Grace Susan Burgess – who had been born in Shanghai. They married on 27 June 1931, and together they had a son and a daughter.

He stayed with the Police for three years and then worked for the Shanghai Gas Company before joining the shipping company Butterfield and Swire. When war broke out with the Japanese, he and his family were interred in a civilian camp where he was put to work in the kitchens. In his own words, he was in the camp for six months and ten days before deciding to escape as he was having serious domestic problems with his wife - and the Japanese had refused to move him to another camp. He escaped by crawling under the barbed wire fence and eventually met up with British forces in south China. (There is a whole chapter devoted to Jack's escape from Shanghai in Hughes' book *Foreign Devil*, although interestingly no mention of his family is made.) In fact he claimed that he preferred the threat of being captured and tortured by the Japanese than spending any more time with his wife.

Many years later, the letter he left for the Camp Commandant before his escape was uncovered in Tokyo and is heartfelt in his grievances about how he suffered at his wife's hands but it is questionable as to how serious their falling out was, and whether he was in fact using it as a smokescreen so that his family would not be punished for his escape. Whatever their relationship, at the end of the war, his wife and two children were successfully liberated from the camp in August 1945 and repatriated to England while Conder decided to live in Hong Kong.

Here, Conder's first job was Manager of the Red Lion in Kowloon, before working at a bar called Victor's, which he then took over and naturally renamed it Conder's Bar. This bar was the one off Queens Road Central that Fleming and Hughes had visited. Found down a narrow, dark side alley, and despite being far from unique, it was certainly one of *the* places to drink in the 1950s – for expats living in Hong Kong and also for visiting military personnel. It promised an English pub atmosphere with Conder billing himself as the 'most popular host in the Far East.' Of course there were many old friends and colleagues from his China days also living in Hong Kong and these too became regulars as well as Freemasons, as he had joined the Shamrock Lodge in 1948, which could be found, somewhat conveniently just around the corner on Queens Road Central. Over the years it also became a favoured haunt of the legal profession.

At some stage, Conder had written this poem:

The Preservation of Man

The horse and mule live thirty years

And nothing know of wines and beers

The goat and sheep at twenty die

With never a taste of bourbon or rye.

The cow drinks water by the ton

And at 18 is mostly done.

The dog at 16 cashes in

Without the aid of rum or gin.

The cat on milk and water soaks

And then in 12 short years it croaks.

The modest, sober, bone dry hen

Lays eggs for nogs, then dies at 10.

All animals are strictly dry

They sinless live and swiftly die.

But sinful, ginful, bourbon-soaked men

Survive for three score years and ten

And some of us, the mighty few,

Stay pickled till we're 92

Fleming described the bar fulsomely, 'We started off our evening at the solidest bar in Hong Kong—the sort of place that Hemingway liked to write about, lined with ships' badges and other trophies, with, over the bar, a stuffed alligator with an iguana riding on its back. The bar belongs to Jack Conder, a former Shanghai municipal policeman and reputed to have been the best pistol shot there in the old days.' This was another of Fleming's inventions as there is no other record suggesting that Conder was a crack shot - remember he is an author of fiction and not a documentarist. He writes to excite the reader. However, there is a link worth mentioning. During the Second World War, Fleming had visited an establishment to train operatives in sabotage and subversion. He was invited to spend a few days there to see how the place worked, and later he noted that a couple of the instructors had served in the Shanghai police - including the firearms expert. No doubt he would have asked Conder is he had known an officer called Murphy.

Fleming said also that Conder sold drinks at reasonable prices, and others noted that the house speciality was a Black and Tan (Worthington draught beer and Manx's Oyster Stout). The establishment was across two floors; in the downstairs bar he did not allow women to drink but they could eat in the restaurant on the first floor.

Unsurprisingly, the bar became the regular meeting place of Alcoholics Synonymous, which had been founded on 5 November 1955. Membership was restricted to 16: Conder was Treasurer,

Hughes a co-founder, and the rest were a mix of press people, businessmen, diplomats, and a few lawyers. Fleming thought there were more press people than other types but whatever they were, he described them as lesser Hemingway characters. One of the members he met was Wendell 'Bud' Merick, an American who had been a war correspondent during the Korean War and then had moved to Hong Kong as Bureau Chief of United Press. Another was Austin Coates, son of the composer Eric Coates, and a Civil Servant and Special Magistrate in the New Territories who, during the War, had served in RAF Intelligence in Asia.

When Fleming flew into town this was the first time for the Alcoholics to meet on a Wednesday night as usually meetings started on a Saturday morning before drifting into a long and leisurely lunch - Conder's sold steaks, chops and other typically hearty food - with conversation that put the world to right continuing late into the afternoon. Fleming of course was by now more than famous and so it was unlikely that the Alcoholics were upset by this change of schedule.

Apparently Conder's sold twelve different types of beer but initiates to Alcoholics Synonymous had to drink sixteen bottles of the locally brewed San Miguel - at least this was what Fleming was told - which Fleming found not to his taste. (For those who have not enjoyed the pleasure of drinking San Miguel it was first brewed in the Philippines in the 1890s and was exported to Hong Kong until the company opened a brewery in the colony in the late 1940s.) As Fleming was not a big beer drinker and the Pilsner style barely existed in 1950s England, it is perhaps unsurprising it was not to his liking.

However, it would seem that Fleming was being gently strung along (most likely by Merick) as new members and their guests (guests were always welcome - but not wives in the early years) did not have to endure an initiation ceremony not least because to become a member one's drinking prowess was readily assumed. In fact the Charter of the Club was clear:

1. To act as a means of gathering its members together at the appointed time and place for the purpose of drinking beverages of alcoholic content.

2. To promote the relief of hangovers acquired in the 24 hours preceding meetings.

3. To encourage members who by accident have not acquired the above malady; to offer consolation to those who have done so.

Another more peripatetic member was the journalist Alan Whicker. He had been coming to Hong Kong (and also Tokyo) since his days as a war correspondent covering the conflict in Korea. After switching to broadcast journalism, he returned to Hong Kong in 1958 for the opening segment of *Whicker's World* (this was when it was part of the BBC's *Tonight* programme) and, according to his autobiography, he always made a visit to the Alcoholics. Other cities he visited in this opening series included Tokyo, Singapore, and Hawaii, and it may have also been the success of *Whicker's World* that prompted the *Sunday Times* to dispatch Fleming on his own tour of the world. As will be seen later, Whicker too becomes part of this story when the film of *You Only Live Twice* was shot.

And is AS still functioning? In 2019 a gathering still meet every second Saturday of the month in the Foreign Correspondents' Club.

TOKYO

From Hong Kong Fleming flew to Tokyo with Hughes on a second BOAC Comet 4 - this one a brand new model registered as G/APDO.

After taking off from Kai Tak, they flew over Taiwan, over the Okinawa islands, and finally over Mount Fuji before they flew into Haneda, then the only international airport serving Tokyo (and indeed had only opened for international flights in 1955). Fleming arrived wary of the Japanese because of the Second World War and the fact that he had friends who had suffered at their hands. He described them as bad enemies but also admitted that Hughes was totally enamoured by the country and the people.

Fleming was not a pioneer when it came to visiting Tokyo from England. For example, the composer Benjamin Britten had made a visit in 1956 and had commented that while he liked the small things in Japan, the large things like cities, the way the Japanese behaved and their thinking 'have all got something wrong.'

Perhaps then Fleming's immediate impression of Tokyo having endless and depressing suburbs was a typical reaction from a British visitor. (Although of course these suburbs have grown ever since and are possibly even more monotonous and depressing.) Drab featureless concrete buildings lined the road, interspersed with factories, dusty wasteland, and junkyards piled with rusting iron and abandoned American cars.

The American occupation of Japan had ended in 1952, and when Fleming and Hughes arrived the country was booming as it marched towards becoming the world's second biggest economy. In food, clothing and housing Western and Japanese styles were thoroughly mixed. Kids jived to jazz, and both local and western pop music was making in-roads.

The two men stayed not in a western hotel - Fleming's preference - but in a *ryokan* which, despite the initial misgivings of a somewhat grumpy middle-aged man, he eventually liked. This was the Fukudaya Inn, not far from Shibuya and still in business today. In fact, the inn had opened in Tokyo during the early years of the 20 century; had burned down in the Great Kanto earthquake of 1923, and had suffered serious damage from the fire bombing of Tokyo in the Second World War. (It was now rebuilt of course.)

Fleming described how it took an hour by taxi to reach the hotel, driving through the suburbs, then darkened side-streets where they had to stop every so often to ask for directions, and then finally bumping along a rutted and dark lane before arriving at a building that reminded him of a villa and surrounded by dwarf pines and shrubs. They had landed at Haneda at 1am and so they did not reach the hotel until well after 2am but they were met by 'two, wide-awake, bowing woman in full traditional dress.'

At the door he had no choice but to remove his shoes and wear a pair of ill-fitting slippers.

To his chintzy English tastes everything in the inn looked too foreign and too delicate. 'I hate small, finicky breakable things,' he wrote. He failed to even understand the form of a Japanese flower arrangement describing it as a spindly branch encrusted with flowers sticking out of a tall rough pottery vase and whatever the message was in their arrangement, he recalled it was hidden from him. T*atami* mats he described morbidly as looking like funeral cards. Perhaps he was just in a belligerent mood.

His description of his room would be familiar to anyone who has stayed in Japan - even in the 21 century: in the centre of the room lay the thin *futon* over which was draped a silk eiderdown. The pillow was hard and small. Next to the bed stood a small teapot, a glass with a wooden cover, a small lacquer box containing toothpicks, and a bed light. He did not mention the presence of an ash tray but of course there would have been one, or maybe two in those days. However he did note the pen and ink that was made available, the charcoal fire that could be laid in a pot, and the lack of storage space.

To help him fall sleep he swallowed a sleeping pill.

Early next morning, awoken by a small earthquake and a giggling maid, his humour had returned.

His agenda was packed and, as he only had three days in Tokyo, Fleming had instructed, 'there would be no politicians, museums, temples, Imperial Palaces or *Noh* plays, let alone tea ceremonies.' The final itinerary had been put together by Hughes and his friend Torao 'Tiger' Saito, a well-respected senior journalist with the *Asahi Shimbun* and who was also responsible for editing the much admired annual English-language almanac called, *This is Japan*. Fleming described him as a chunky reserved man, with a considerable store of humorous stories, and the look of a fighting man.

His first engagement was a gossipy Tiffin lunch at the Imperial Hotel with fellow author Somerset Maugham, who was visiting Japan for the first time in thirty years, along with his secretary and companion Alan Searle. Whereas Fleming had flown, Maugham had sailed via the Suez Canal. Maugham was then in his mid-eighties, frail and slightly forgetful but nonetheless after Tokyo he planned to visit Kyoto for two weeks not least because he was then a popular writer among Japanese students. (Far more so than in England where he admitted he was now largely ignored.) His plan was to visit universities, sip tea with the professors, and sign a lot of books.

They talked maliciously about friends in London, and more lovingly about Fleming's wife - who Maugham, according to Fleming, wished to marry. In fact despite his homosexuality Maugham had always been open about his admiration for Fleming's wife Anne, calling her once, 'the Madame de Sevigne of our day.'

Despite Maugham's age, there was no afternoon nap in the offing as Fleming insisted that they all visit the Kodokan Judo Institute, the headquarters of the global Judo sport. Not only did they see regular training sessions but also a mock fight between girls. Both Fleming and Maugham were fascinated and delighted by what they witnessed and Fleming described it at length in his article.

Fleming was insistent that he meets a fortune-teller, not because he was that interested in what he called 'sooth-saying' but because he was intrigued by all matters connected with extra-sensory perception. A session with the supposedly much admired Seki Ryushi was arranged for the late afternoon. Despite asking for the appointment, Fleming was skeptical and afterwards said that it told him absolutely nothing other than he was an independent spirt, that he would live until he was 80, that he would return to Japan, and that he looked more like his mother than his father. He was also told he should stop being obstinate to his wife.

Later when it came to writing his article, Fleming included a wry reference to a second fortune teller - a friend of Seki-san - who had failed to foretell his own death. On 25 November 25 about two weeks after Fleming had left Tokyo, Sozan Takashima was stabbed to death by an assassin, a young jealous colleague in the same profession.

He, Saito and Hughes ate dinner in the Ginza, consuming what he admitted were vast quantities of *sashimi* and hot *sake*. As all visitors find, Fleming discovered that the daytime ugliness of Tokyo would vanish come night time to be replaced by a cityscape of sizzling neon colours.

The next day, Saito returned to work while Fleming and Hughes indulged in the soothing pleasures of a Tokyo *sento* to sweat out their hangovers. He called it the Tokyo Onsen - a place that is not now identifiable by name - and it was not an *onsen* (which uses water piped from deep volcanic springs) but a bath house using heated water from the main supply. All we know is that it was a large drab building but then most were.

Here Fleming paid 15 shillings and was pampered by a girl who told him her name was Baby, who he described as a smaller version of Bridget Bardot dressed in the shortest and tightest of white shorts and a white bra, and the prettiest girl he saw during the length of his stay. His session took place in a private room where he was told to undress before taking a Turkish bath, followed by a scrub and shampoo, a soak in hot water for ten minutes, and then finally a deep massage. However nothing untoward occurred because in that establishment it didn't. (Or at least not with Fleming.)

By now, two weeks into his world trip, Fleming had decided that he understood how people viewed sex in the Far East: simply stated a delightful pastime unconnected with sin. (And on that he was right.) It was no doubt an attitude that he would appreciate. Certainly in his younger days, he had a ruthless attitude towards women and was, to say the least, promiscuous leaving a trail of distressed damsons behind. He was also no prude, was said to be almost obsessively interested in sex, and would be upfront about his desires with a woman who he found attractive.

Some years later in a conversation with the ex-CIA Director, Allen Dulles, he is asked what is his ideal woman? After musing on the delights of WRENS, he says 'I like the fact that they want to please. To make one happy. Rather like you know, if you have ever been to Japan; there's a desire to please among Orientals, which I find very pleasant after living in the harsh West.'

Fleming then strolled through the busy Ginza, walking the streets, window shopping, and finally buying a woodblock print of a man being beheaded - he noted that Tokyo was already the most expensive city in the world and this was confirmed by the prices he saw. It was here too that he was approach by pimps who offered a rich palette of pleasures, all to be discovered down nearby side streets. They overwhelmed him: ten for every one that he would find in Paris, he wrote. Hughes said it was the same everywhere and with everything: too many pimps, too many whores, too many taxi drivers, too many shop assistants, too many people flocking to Tokyo desperate to make a living.

On the second night, Fleming, Hughes and Saito dined in a private room in a restaurant hard by the Shinbashi Bridge. Entertained by *geisha,* they ate fish including an eel soup that Fleming thoroughly enjoyed. This gathering would later become the basis of the opening scene in *You Only Live Twice,* and the two *geisha* in attendance would become Trembling Leaf and Grey Pearl. Perhaps having picked up some tips from the fortune teller, Fleming read his *geisha's* palm. (NB: Somerset Maugham had written a book called *The Trembling of a Leaf* published in 1921.)

Afterwards Fleming insisted on another drink and they found a legion of small colourful bars in the crowded lantern-hung lanes.

On the way back to the *ryoken,* they passed the newly built Tokyo Tower that had risen spectacularly above the city's rooftops but not without its critics. Some said it had sprung up with no heed to the local environment whereas the Eiffel Tower was an integral part of a city plan. Others complained that indeed it was just a copy of the Eiffel Tower, uglier to boot and the owners should have constructed something original.

Remember this was 1959. Japan could see nothing wrong in outright copying the best of the West. The girls, Fleming noted, aped the West in many ways not least the desire to have long legs achieved by wearing the highest of stiletto heels with a couple of inches added to a girl's height by adopting hair-dos that were now permanent waves or frizzy mops. They were also undergoing surgery to remove the Mongolian fold of their eyelids and to widen their eyes.

He also noted how calm everyone was despite living in a city that was over-crowded, with *kamikaze* taxi drivers, and where many people were still fighting for a decent living.

But Tokyo was changing fast and the young generation saw that they could take advantage of this change and start to define it. For example, in terms of music, Japanese pop music had made an impact, dominated though by sentimentally written and performed songs. The most popular when Fleming arrived was *Nangoku Tosa*, an old Shikoku folk song performed by Peggy Hayama. She had been born in 1933 and as a schoolgirl became a fan of American jazz when she listened to the armed forces radio of the occupying American troops. She joined an amateur jazz band and started singing at the US base in Yokohama. Quickly she became a huge hit with the troops and then went on to become one of Japan's leading popular singers.

Foreign singers were also gaining in popularity with *Smoke gets in your Eyes* by The Platters being successful in 1959 but theme songs and soundtrack recordings were even more popular such as *I'll remember tonight* sung by Pat Boone and *Rio Brave* by Dean Martin.

More popular in Japan than back in England was French *chanson* and while the French lyrics was not understood, the romantic mood of the songs clearly struck a chord. The monthly magazine *Chanson* found that the most popular French singers in Japan included Yves Montand (who was due to visit Tokyo a few weeks after Fleming had left), Juliette Greco, Gilbert Becaud, Line Renaud, and Jacqueline Francois.

The local movie business was thriving with over 500 films produced annually - although many were poor quality. In part the volume was in response to the rise of TV's popularity where there were over 3 million sets, a number that was growing rapidly.

In terms of technology the likes of Sanyo and Sony were already selling transistor radios that could be held comfortably in the hand.

Where Tokyo lagged behind was in the provision of hotels. (Just like Hong Kong.) Many were often fully occupied as both tourists and business visitors alike were flocking to Tokyo and, because of the demand, there was very much a take-it or leave it attitude at the reception desk. This would change a few years later when the looming Olympics led to a rash of hotels being built and service improved immeasurably.

The morning after their *geisha* experience they caught a train to the ancient spa town of Yugawara where they stayed in a simple Japanese *ryokan* facing the broad expanse of Sagami Bay.

The next day they started out for the Fujiya Hotel, located in the village of Miyanoshita, a not to distant taxi ride away.

At the Fujiya he was pleased to see a photo of his great uncle on display - the hotel manager was President of the International Moustache Club founded at the Fujiya in 1931, and Fleming's great uncle was renowned for his two-foot long facial hair. (To become a member the uncle had to send an autographed photo of his beard and moustache to the hotel. The membership was worldwide and at the time of Uncle Fleming joining in the 1930s numbered members from Japan the UK, Siam, India, Germany and Java albeit only seventeen in number. Other British members included Lord Wyfold and S G Brinkley but I have been unable to confirm the name of the uncle.)

The present hotel opened in 1891 and was built using an amalgam of traditional Japanese and western styles. Many famous visitors had stayed included Lefcadio Hearn, Charlie Chaplin, Prince Albert (later George VI) of the UK, the Swedish Crown Prince and his retinue, and the Emperor Showa.

At the time of their visit the rate was Y2000 for a single room with bath. If Fleming had stayed in a Suite he could have paid up to Y6,000. It was not mentioned as to whether they took lunch at the hotel but that would have cost them Y1000 each.

That same day they returned to Tokyo in what Fleming said was the most beautiful streamlined aluminium train, painted orange and belonging to the Odawara Express Train Company (the original name but by 1959 known officially as the Odakyu Electric Railway Company). Inside they listened to gentle piped music and admired the pretty girls who dispensed green tea and Japanese whiskey.

Called the *Romancecar* because of the design of the paired seats without separating arm rests, this was a relatively new train service, having started in 1957 and was very popular not just among young lovers.

This brought the chapter to an end. Whether Fleming had changed his opinion about the Japanese he did not say but his tone is positive and it would appear that other than his visit to the fortune-teller, everything was enjoyable, although he provides no overarching description of the city.

For this we need to turn to James Kirkcup, the English writer, poet and academic who went to Japan in 1959 as he had gained a teaching position at Tohoku University, Sendai.

'Everywhere people were walking, trotting, running, cycling, driving along helter-skelter on tiny three-wheeled trucks; there was a lorry load of blue-bloomered, apple-cheeked working women with white cloths draped round their heads, smiling and waving at me; there were sturdy blue-jeaned boys with white towels knotted round their shaven pates and riding rickety bicycles, holding the handlebars with only one muscular brown hand, while the other bore aloft above the right shoulder a tall pile of trays and dishes and bowls full of noodles and steaming soup. Farther on there were women in kimono and wooden pattens, pattering along, carrying rosy-faced babies on their backs, wrapped in padded, quilted, flowery capes...Everything was sharp, quick, keen, a little too hectic. It was like looking at a speeded-up film. And the noise was deafening.'

(This appeared in *These Horned Islands*, which was one of the books on Japan that Fleming admired and later used as a reference when it came to writing *You Only Live Twice*.)

At the end of Fleming's chapter on Tokyo could be found various recommendations to help the visitor find accomodation or enjoy an evening's entertainment.

For an exotic night on the town it was recommended to visit the Copacabana run by Madam Cherry (a pre-war dance hostess in Shanghai) where the hostesses were from Kobe which, in Western opinion at the time, was the cradle of the most beautiful Japanese girls; it would cost Y1,000 (about a £1) an hour to enjoy their company and they would gently ply the guests with snacks and drinks in dimly lit booths. The club was renowned for being the most sophisticated and exclusive club in Tokyo and was to be found in Akasaka. Here too secret and often corrupt business deals would be gently teased out over the cocktails. Otherwise two cheaper option were the L'Espoir where the *mama-san* was known as Beautiful Crystal, and Onsome run by Dawn of Light. *Gaijin* we were told 'are discreetly and carefully screened before being allowed in.'

Fleming also wrote that if he had not stayed in the Japanese inn, the hotel of choice in Tokyo was the Imperial Hotel (where he had met Maugham), which cost £6 a night for a regular room. Other recommended hotels included the Shiba Park which was close to Tokyo Tower, cheaper as a room cost £3, and a hotel favoured by visiting rugby teams, and the Nikkatsu, which was the first luxury hotel to be opened after the Second World War.

The Matsudaira, situated then on the outskirts of Tokyo was said to be quiet and discreet, and had expansive grounds as the hotel was formerly the residence of Lord Matsudaira. It catered for foreign airline crews on stop-overs.

For eating, the recommendations included the Prunier restaurant, and for fish the Tsujitome run by Kaichi Tsuji, and a long established *kaiseki* restaurant. For *tempura*, the Hashizen in Shimbashi was recommended. (Up until recently this could be found at 1-7-11 Shinbashi, Minato but it has now closed down.)

And, although he did not eat there, it was noted that the ancient and famed Momonjiya restaurant still served roast monkey, monkey brains and wild boar.

On Friday 13 November, Fleming caught a JAL flight to Hawaii - leaving Hughes to return to Hong Kong - having eaten a last and 'melancholy' supper of fish and martinis with his friend. There is no doubt the two men had enjoyed each other's friendship and company.

In all, Fleming was away for five weeks. Back in England, the articles were written up, published, and became a big success. Leonard Russell, the *Sunday Times* editor, sent a note congratulating Fleming and making the comment that Fleming has come across as a 'unique and endearing eccentric.'

Fleming also arranged to leave the *Sunday Times,* and then rented office space at 4 Old Mitre Court off Fleet Street, with the telephone number Ludgate Circus 8655.

SOMERSET MAUGHAM

Since the publication of the First Edition, I have found more detail about Maugham's visit to Japan and his extended contact with the country. This I felt deserves a short section but can be skipped for those who have little or no interest in the man.

Maugham at one stage was one of the most celebrated and fashionable of twentieth century English writers. Indeed his success had started back in the late 19 century with the publication of his first novel *Lisa of Lambeth* that led to him giving up his medical career to become a full-time novelist.

During the First World War he was recruited into the British Secret Intelligence Service. Subsequently Maugham used his spying experience to write *Ashenden: Or the British Agent*, a collection of short stories about a spy. It is claimed that this had some influence on Fleming when he came to create James Bond.

Maugham's reputation though comes from the books he wrote depicting life in the British colonies and more specifically the troubled lives of ex-pats trapped in an existence that they could not escape from.

His first visit to Japan was in 1917, when he was sent on a mission to Russia to find ways that the British Government could support the provisional government of Alexander Kerensky. At this time, with the War going on in Europe the only way to enter Russia was via Japan. Later this journey would find its way into one of the Ashenden stories.

After the War he made further short visits but these were never translated into either the novels or travel books that became Maugham's stock in trade.

His one story set in the country involves a British ex-pat living in Kobe who tells the story of a second ex-pat who was living in Yokohama. However it is a generic story that could have been set in any of the colonies or great trading cities of the Far East.

Sometimes Japan and the Japanese were mentioned in passing but these mentions were scattered and it would hard to claimed that Maugham as a novelist was a Nipponphile.

However in the 1950s, Maugham's works suddenly became immensely popular in Japan, possibly because his troubled characters mirrored some of the issues that the Japanese themselves faced in the immediate post-War years.

This visit in 1959 was at a time when he was famous in Japan but with a reputation that was declining in England, a state that Maugham was more than aware of as he had recently commented that when he stayed in London 'no one gives a damn that I am there.'

An exhibition of photographs, manuscripts and memorabilia had now been mounted in Tokyo in his honour, and he was invited to its opening.

He took the French liner SS *Laos* and the route was a veritable nostalgia fest for Maugham as they sailed via Aden, Bombay, Colombo, Singapore, Saigon, Manila and Hong Kong before landing at Yokohama.

He was at this time a greater celebrity than Fleming, and was pursued by crowds of people who wanted to see the great man. In fact he spent much of this time within the Imperial Hotel because of this, although he did visit some tourist sights.

He also travelled to Kyoto where he was escorted by the novelist Francis King to see *Noh* theatre, and to enjoy a *geisha* party. King noted that while Maugham tired easily, he had sat all afternoon on the floor watching the performance. In total, he stayed in Japan for thirty days.

Another British novelist to visit Japan in the same year was Sacheverell Sitwell who wrote about his trip in *The Bridge of the Brocade Sash*. He noted how rapidly Japan was changing and that much was being lost but he hoped that this was for the better for Japan's burgeoning population. He thought he had visited at the right time but was gracious enough to note that perhaps the new Japan 'may not be less sensational.'

TOKYO 1962

Not only had Fleming's account of his first visit appeared in the Sunday Times in early 1960 but he also wrote an article entitled *'Spy Writer's Reconnaissance in Japan'* for *This is Japan* 1961 (but actually published in September 1960).

In this version there are a number of differences from the chapter published in *Thrilling Cities*. Mostly these are further explanatory remarks around events (*Thrilling Cities* was clearly edited to shorten it) but there is one significant difference: the girl in the bathhouse that Fleming visited is called Kissy rather than Baby. And Kissy is the name given to the Japanese heroine in *You Only Live Twice.* So why would Fleming not use Kissy for the version that appeared in *Thrilling Cities*?

What we learn from *This is Japan* is that shortly after his first visit in 1959, Fleming had already decided to set a James Bond novel in Japan so perhaps when *Thrilling Cities* was published he did not wish to expose his inspiration for the name and so changed it. Perhaps it was the girl's real name and he decided that some prudence was required.

However despite having chosen Japan as a setting, his next books were to be *Thunderball, The Spy Who Loved Me,* and *On Her Majesty's Secret Service,* none of which featured Japan at all. However *Thunderball* and *On Her Majesty's Secret* along with *You Only Live Twice* were to form the Blofeld trilogy - the arch villain and

Bond's nemesis.

By the middle of 1962, he was planning his second visit to Japan. He had written and edited *On Her Majesty's Secret Service*, the book was being prepared for publication, and already Fleming knew that the his next novel would definitely continue the storyline and possibly bring the battle between Bond and Blofeld to a conclusion.

He would be coming to a Japan that was changing fast not only economically but with an increasing influx of cultural influences hitherto little seen in the country. For example, at an exhibition called 'Experiments in Modern Art' one artist claimed that a black coffin, stuffed with a stalactite grotto made of cement represented the *Secret Rite of Death and Eros*. As elsewhere there were seeds of rebellion in the air but not only from disaffected youth but by workers too. Some of this was a reaction against the so-called 'huge growth' edict of the Government who was urging all citizens to prioritise economic growth across all aspects of their lives; the Government too was assessing what industries would have strong future (electronics being one) and which were likely to fail - such as textiles - because of competition elsewhere. This was a different Japan to the one he had visited only three years earlier.

The Treaty of Mutual Cooperation and Security between the United States and Japan, first signed in 1952 had been renewed in 1960 - this being the document that allowed the US to have a heavy military presence in Japan on the proviso that she defend Japan against any foreign aggression. This led to 175,000 men and women protesting in Tokyo against what they saw as Japan coming under continued control of the US. In 1962 there was still distrust. 'Yankees go home.' was their chant.

If there was an air of radicalism emerging, conversely Tokyo had established itself as leading centre in the world of classical music. Its orchestras were respected and Japan acted as a host for the best in the world.

Tokyo, though, was becoming increasingly dominated by Western icons - or more precisely Americanisation. Visitors from abroad were often disappointed when they first arrived as they searched in vain for the oriental mystery and exotic atmosphere that they imagined would be found in abundance. They would have to scratch hard at the surface to find old Japanese customs and thoughts.

On the TV it was said there was an over reliance on American TV shows and films. Frank Sinatra came to Japan and appeared for two evenings at the newly-opened Mikado Theatre-restaurant, with the 2,500 seats priced at Y5,000 selling out immediately.

Stereo record players were becoming all the rage, and the number of records pressed had doubled since Fleming was last in Tokyo. Of the 6,000 different LP titles, over fifty per cent were foreign. They cost Y2,000 and a small stereo player cost Y25,000.

Juliette Greco had now become the most popular *chansonesse* in Japan, and she and other French singers has a major influence on Japanese popular song writing.

Affecting everything in Tokyo - and not necessarily in a good way - was the preparations for the 1964 Olympic Games. One of the worst problems afflicting the capital was the traffic and so a mammoth road-building programme was underway as well as the construction of the athletic facilities including the expansion of the national athletic ground to become the Olympic Stadium with a capacity of 100,000, and the construction of a national gymnasium holding 16,000 people.

Cheering the populace on was a national campaign called 'Let us raise Rising Sun flags in the Tokyo Olympics.' The use of the Rising Sun flag was controversial as the *hinomaru* was seen as being a symbol of Japan's militaristic past but overall most people saw the Olympics as something prestigious and a demonstration of Japan's increasing role globally.

Alongside all this activity was the building of Japan's first *Shinkansen* line between Tokyo and Osaka, at a length of 500 kilometres. The trains would run at 200km per hour but were already being tested to exceed this speed.

Fleming could already buy miniaturised radios when he first came to Japan but now Sony and Mitsubishi were selling micro TVs with 5 and 6 inch screens. Japan was fast becoming a nation of gadgets.

Tokyo's population was in excess of 10 million and was expanding by around 300,000 annually as more and more people poured in for work.

After only three years absence, Fleming was certainly going to see a difference when he arrived, and perhaps already he was feeling that his creation was an anachronism in this new world where the young were gaining there own voice and the pace of change was ferocious.

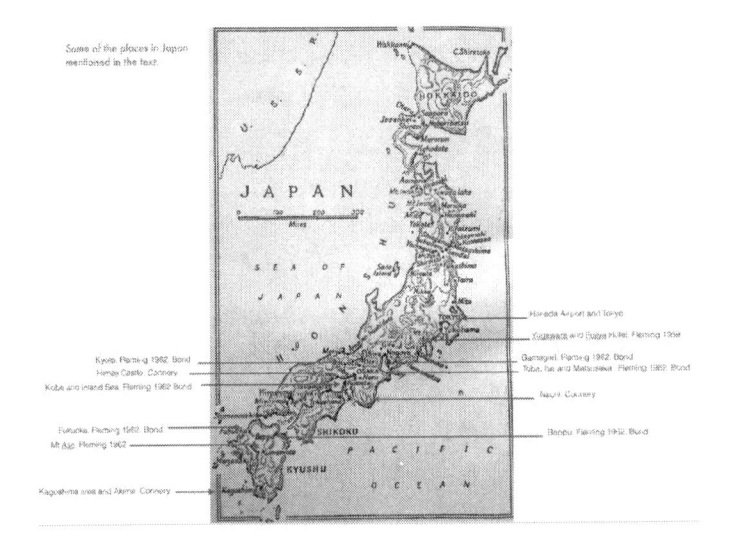

Some of the places in Japan mentioned in the text.

FLEMING VISITS JAPAN, 1962

Failing health and strength;

My teeth grate

On the sand in the seaweed.

BASHO

The purpose of Fleming's second trip was solely to research factual details, more local colour and inspiration for *You Only Live Twice*. Having already conceived an outline plot, he spent two weeks touring Japan, accompanied again by Richard Hughes and Torao 'Tiger' Saito with all their costs being paid for by Fleming's company, Glidrose Productions. He arrived in mid November 1962, a few weeks after the London film premiere of *Dr No*, which he had attended. (The film was not released in Japan until the middle of 1963.)

In his book *Foreign Devil*, Hughes wrote that Fleming had sent a letter before arriving,

Graham Thomas

Dear Dikko,

I have it in mind that James Bond's next adventure shall be in Japan, and although I have been reading up some excellent books on that excellent country, notably by James Kirkup and Fosco Maraini, I find that I can't get any further without coming back...After perhaps a couple of days in Tokyo, I would like to take the most luxurious modern train down south to the Inland Sea and beyond to whatever bizarre corner of Japan you and Tiger can think up...'

He went on to say that he wanted the heroine of the book to be a beautiful *ama* (a pearl diver) that it would feature volcanoes, and a castle where a mad foreigner would live.

Fleming's research for the Bond novels was always meticulous – either undertaking it himself, reading books, or asking experts for advice. He had a natural eye for detail hence, although he had previously visited Japan, he wanted to update his knowledge of the country and to understand aspects of the culture in greater depth. (As Hughes described it, Fleming set out to seek spiritual inspiration and carnal knowledge.)

One expert that Fleming turned to was the aforementioned Kirkup, a friend since 1943 when, during an air raid Fleming went into a pub off Piccadilly, started talking to a fellow drinker who turned out to be the poet James Kirkup.

He had also asked for advice from William Plomer, his friend, mentor and editor at Cape before leaving, asking for tips and advice. Plomer, an author and poet in his own right, had lived in Japan for several years during the 1920s where he had a relationship with a Japanese man. In fact a young and admiring Fleming had written a fan letter to Plomer in the 1920s and had met with him when Plomer returned from Tokyo in 1929. It was he who advised Fleming to buy Maraini and Kirkup's book on Japan - if Fleming wasn't already considering these. Plomer himself had written about Japan in his autobiography *Double Lives* and had concluded that to live successfully as a foreigner in Japan he had to hide if not discard his former life and live as a local – hence living a double life or perhaps living twice.

We know that Fleming had decided to write a Bond novel set in Japan after his first visit but then put the idea to one side. Now Fleming was planning the book when Japan was very much at the forefront of the West's mind not least as she was about to host the Tokyo Olympic Games. She was a country too that had fully emerged from post-War defeat to becoming a major economic power. Her goods were starting to infiltrate the West and the moniker 'Made in Japan' was beginning to mean more than just cheap plastic or tin trash.

Maybe he decided to ride this wave of interest and Japan, as he knew from his previous visit, was decidedly exotic and the perfect place for Bond to exercise his charms. On the other hand public opinion worldwide was still mixed about Japan. Even a decade later in 1971, the State Visit of Emperor Hirohito to England was deeply resented by a swathe of the population.

It has also been suggested that Fleming was increasingly aware of his own mortality following a heart attack, that he wished to take the opportunity to revisit favourite parts of the world, and to meet old friends for possibly the last time.

When Fleming flew into Haneda for the second time he had become a globally recognised celebrity and was whisked through immigration and customs. In a biography it says he played the part to the full: puffing on his Moreland cigarettes, carrying a shooting stick and wearing his signature light-weight blue suit, blue polka-dot bow tie, and slip-on shoes. (The latter being an excellent choice as it would save having to bend down and fiddle with the laces every time they needed to be removed which, of course, would be frequent in Japan where shoes are always taken off before entering a house.)

He had been met by Hughes and Saito and they took a cab into

Tokyo, which cost Y1500, at a time when the Yen was worth around Y360 to the $ and Y1,008 to the £.

Unlike his first visit Fleming was able to stay in a western-style hotel, the brand new Hotel Okura: a first class hotel with western rooms and beds; the hotel boasted in their advertising of having 550 rooms with TV and radio, a Japanese spa and a Turkish Bath.

The hotel had opened a few months before Fleming arrived, anticipating that the economic boom was unstoppable and that significant business would come from the Tokyo Olympics. Its competition for the top spot was the regal Imperial Hotel that had ruled unchallenged for decades. This was about to change, and in fact over thirty hotels were now Western style.

With a burst of inspiration, Kishichiro Okura, Okura's owner, brought together an imaginative group of individuals in the late 1950s with a brief to combine both Western modern and traditional Japanese elements in the design. That group included the architects Yoshiro Taniguchi and Hideo Kosaka, the artist Shiko Munakata and the potter Kenkichi Tomimoto. Together they moulded a unique design - that used the indigenous colours, textures, and materials of Japan within a Modernistic flourish - into a masterpiece that could never be reproduced again.

After staying in Tokyo for two nights the three men then left for a journey that would take them to Gamagori, Kyoto, the Inland Sea, and finally Kyushu before returning to Tokyo.

The weather was perfect as it was late autumn and they were treated to the splendid colours of leaves turning gold, the rice fields deep green, and that wonderful clear azure sky special to Japan at that time of year.

The first leg of the journey saw them board an early morning express train to Gamagori on the Tokaido Line where, some three hours later, they checked-in at the Gamagori Hotel. Opened in 1912, this distinguished and pretty hotel stood three floors high and was roofed with sparkling green tiles. Their front facing rooms overlooked the calm Mikawa Bay with superb views of Takeshima Island, the Yaotomi Shrine and other small islands. Members of the Japanese royal family were among the guests who had stayed over the years. Rooms cost Y900 - Y7,000 without a meal, and the hotel boasted a golf course and a table tennis room.

By now Hughes and Saito had learned Fleming's working methods: the day was usually given over to travel and sight-seeing. If he had a thought or wanted to record something he would write it down in a small notepad. Back at the hotel in the evening, he would spend a couple of hours before dinner writing up his notes in a loose-leaf soft covered notebook. The Japanese for 'top secret' *gokuhi* was one word he wrote down.

Next morning they ate a Western-style buffet, though not before Hughes puffed his way through one of his cheap cigars, his way of starting every morning. Fleming observed that when the Japanese used a knife and fork, rather than following the American way, which was to first cut and then pick up the food one-handed with a fork - which might have been expected - they used both hands for knife and fork.

Packed and with the bill settled, they took a taxi from Gamagori to Irago, a small port further round the Mikawa Bay on the Atsumi Peninsula. From here a hydrofoil called the *Pearl Queen* ran a swift trip to Mikimoto's pearl fisheries on a small island off Toba.

Mikimoto Kokichi was the man who had succeeded in producing cultured pearls here in the 1890s and over the decades had created a global business. In 1951, he renamed the island Mikimoto Pearl Island, and develop it for tourism - as he moved the actual oyster farms further south. A commemorative museum to Mikimoto was established in 1958 (he had died in 1954), and a Pearl Museum had newly opened in 1962.

Graham Thomas

As he had written to Hughes, Fleming wanted to seek out the *ama*, the pearl divers, for himself. Of course what he was watching was nothing more than a tourist show but he happily observed the girls dive for pearls and when one came close after leaving the water, he gently touched her shoulder as he wanted to understand what the texture of their wet skin was like. (He was being meticulous in finding out background detail!)

Show over, the three stopped in Toba overnight. That evening, they took a car to a restaurant on the Shima Peninsula where they ate a meal that included a large live lobster, which had Fleming gaping horrified as the twitching creature edged its way off the plate.

The next day their first stop was the Ise shrine, one of the most important in the Shinto religion, and most likely founded in the 5 century AD. Since that time, the most revered shrine building, the Divine Palace, has been rebuilt every twenty years. It was then and still is dedicated to Amaterasu-Omikami, the ancestral *kami* (deity) of the Imperial family and is often referred to as the Soul of Japan.

Another short drive took them north to Matsusaka. Here they stopped at a cattle farm where Fleming was able to massage the cattle by spitting large amounts of *shochu* over the animal's flank and then rubbing it in with a hard brush. All to aid the making of the local *wagyu* beef. (Matsusaka is the least well-known of the best *wagyu* beefs, even in Japan. It enjoys a meatier taste over rivals such as Kobe and Ohmi beef.)

However, cattle having their flanks spat on and massaged is a rather romantic myth used to encourage the notion that the beef is special because of this loving care. In truth, this is not the case: sometimes special show-cattle do have their hide's sheen enhanced by rubbing in *shochu* or *sake*, and sometimes the cattle are massaged as they are kept in pens and this helps them move around but the quality of the beef is down to genetics, their everyday diet, and not to any other external factors.

Having tasted *wagyu* beef cooked by the farmer, they embarked on a gentle 60km drive to Kyoto.

I have seen it suggested that *en-route* they stopped at the city Iga Ueno, and that its castle became the inspiration for the *ninja* training facility. I can find no evidence to support this idea. Neither Fleming or Hughes mentioned the city in any writing, it would have involved a detour from their route, and they had a packed schedule that day. On the other hand the *Iga-ryū* - a historical school of ninjutsu - was based there some hundreds of years previously, and although not located in the city, *Togakure-ryū*, another ancient school of *ninja* was based in the Prefecture, and so the area they were driving through was steeped in *ninja* history. Fleming mentions both schools in the novel.

What is definitively known is that before reaching their hotel they stopped on the outskirts of Kyoto and, for a two hours, explored Nijo Jin-ya. Originally, this was one of a number of historic guest houses where the *daimyo* lords, visiting the Emperor would stay.

From the outside it looked like a typical Edo-style house: surrounded by a plaster and wooden wall, with an outer entrance that led to a small courtyard.

In order to safeguard the *daimyo*, the main building was designed so that it would be difficult for an assassin to reach the guest rooms. False doors, walls and ceilings, trapdoors, spy holes, secret rooms, and death-drops were incorporated into the structure. From the entrance, a 'nightingale floor' was incorporated into the main corridor so that the boards squeaked loudly if they were trodden on.

In Kyoto they stayed at the Miyako Hotel where they checked-in before visiting a bordello in the Shimabara district, the ancient red light area of the city.

Here, Fleming carefully noted the number of bedrooms and worked out how many *ronin* could have eaten in the kitchen while their lords feasted on earthly delights upstairs. He was also interested in the toilet procedures, and had the curator explain them in detail.

They only stayed overnight before driving from Kyoto to Kobe, a short journey. On the way they stopped at a teahouse near Mount Arashiyama. The name was not recorded but it was possibly the Hirano-ya, a four hundred year old teahouse and restaurant. Once in Kobe, they quickly boarded a steamship that would take them through the Seto Inland Sea to Beppu, a journey that would be completed in twelve hours. During the voyage, Tiger mused about opening a hotel on one of the Inland Sea's many islands, and apparently Fleming offered three inspired names for this hotel.

In the 1960s, eight of these ships plied daily across the Seto Inland Sea allowing travellers to easily get from the great conurbation of Osaka and Kobe (and the bigger Kanto region) to Kyushu. The sailing would take fourteen hours; plenty of time to relax, drink, smoke and enjoy a conversation.

Within the James Bond canon, Kyushu is significant as it is here that most of the action takes place in *You Only Live Twice*. Here Fleming would see the spitting hot mud and the deadly volcano that would inspire his creation of an evil garden. It is in the coastal city of Beppu where a reluctant Bond eats the almost translucent flesh of the deadly fugu fish; and lurking in northern Kyushu we find none other than Ernst Stavro Blofeld – using the alias Doctor Shatterhand – who has built an evil castle and deadly garden with the sole intent of encouraging as many Japanese as possible to commit suicide. Kyushu too was described by Stephen Spender the poet and a friend of Fleming's as being 'an ugly place filled with people of almost unrelieved ugliness.' He had visited in 1958. Had he passed on this thought to Fleming?

Beppu is a small city, squashed between the coast and the mountains, and with a population of just over 100,000. Famous for its hot springs that originate thousands of meters underground, it is claimed that more hot springs gush from the earth here than anywhere else in the world. It is these waters and their medicinal qualities that have drawn visitors from all over Japan for centuries. Historically the columns of scalding steam, and the boiling pools of mud would have created a terrifying landscape but like any place that attracted visitors this would have been mixed with all the bawdy fun and pleasure that Japan was famous for, and which was still true when the three travellers arrived.

Like many a tourist town in the 1960s, Beppu had its fair share of strip shows, prostitutes touting for business on street corners, and garish hostess bars. In fact it had more than its fair share, as Beppu was well known for its nightlife, a characteristic that had only been heightened as a result of it being used as a camp and R&R resort by the American occupation forces post Second World War. These bars, soapland establishments, dance halls and jazz clubs all remained long after the Americans had departed.

Beppu too had been spared the US carpet bombing in the last days of the war, and Fleming would have found a city that had retained much of its traditional character albeit now dotted with new landmarks such as the Beppu Tower, a short version of the famous Tokyo Tower.

Despite or perhaps because of this, Beppu itself it is only briefly but accurately described by Hughes in his memoirs as being 'vulgar, amusing and lascivious.'

And that's it. Unfortunately we do not know what the threesome got up to during their overnight stay but most likely Fleming and co. did visit the boiling hot geysers and ponds known as the Beppu Hells as they are later described in the novel. One of these geysers is called Umi Jigoku and from a distance looks like a large and rather pretty pond under a leafy bank. However, closer to it can be seen that the water is boiling with great force and many people in the past have committed suicide by leaping in and being instantly scalded to death. This obviously matched Fleming's desire to visit '...any terrifying manifestation of the horrific in Japan.'

Neither are we told where they stayed in Beppu but it seems unlikely that Fleming slept in a simple ryokan (which is where he sent Bond). As Hughes wrote, '(Fleming) never cared for eating or sleeping on the tatami (floor mats).' Instead I would wager a guess that they checked into one of a number of hotels with Western facilities. These included the Oniyama and Shiragikuso but the one I think most likely is the Suginoi Hotel - but only on the assumption that this was the most expensive.

From Beppu, Fleming, Hughes and Saito head inland finding the scenery dramatically different from much of Japan as it was stark, almost treeless, and formed into strangely shaped undulating hills.

Fleming initially had the idea to include a storyline about the Japanese committing suicide by jumping into a 'live volcano.' He had the idea that perhaps this was where the villian would set up his headquarters. Kyushu was the perfect place for uncovering the factual detail on this as in its centre is the active volcano Mount Aso and, in the decades after the Second World War, it was a popular place for suicides.

To reach the crater they took a ropeway where they could then stand on the crater's rim and look down on the stunning turquoise magna, a sheer drop below.

The ropeway (or cable car) had started operating in 1958 and saved them having to walk to the crater but magnificent as it was, the volcano fails to feature in the novel, and the story of the suicides is conflated with Beppu's Hells to become a deadly aspect of Shatterhand's gardens.

The reason behind this was simple: Fleming realised that attempting to have his villian set up his HQ here was stretching credibility too thinly. This was a barren and exposed landscape with no buildings. Nor shelter or cover. Impossible for an outsider to infiltrate.

They stayed one night in the nearby Aso Kanko Hotel, chosen for straightforward reasons: it was the only Western hotel in the area (and, as we know, Fleming liked his Western trappings); it was celebrated not least because Emperor Hirohito had been a guest as well as other celebrities, and it was expensive and well-appointed.

The hotel had originally opened in the late 1930s as a luxury resort. Immediately after the Second World War it was requisitioned as a R&R centre for the American Eighth Army, and this role continued until the Korean War. In July 1953 the hotel was extensively damaged by a landslide caused by heavy rains, and was subsequently rebuilt in a more contemporary style.

From the hotel they continued on to Fukuoka that, without explaining why, they found anti-climatic. Perhaps exhaustion had set in after their long journey from Tokyo or perhaps they expected a smaller version of Tokyo and were disappointed. Perhaps they were experiencing the same reaction as Stephen Spender had on his trip to Kyushu.

Back in 1962 Fukuoka was far more industrial than it is now because of the nearby coal mining industry. Contemporary accounts describe a city that was dirty, with many unpaved side streets but overflowing with traffic from bicycles, pedestrians, three-wheeled trucks, street vendors pushing carts, and taxis all of which took little notice of traffic laws. Hughes writes that they should have gone to Nagasaki but as the plot line in the novel involves the transformation of Bond into a Japanese miner (more in Chapter 10) it seems probable that Fleming had already come up with this reasonably credible idea, and had known that Fukuoka was at the heart of the mining industry.

Since that time Fukuoka has undergone a miraculous transformation and is now one of Japan's largest and most dynamic cities with outstanding food, much culture, and an eclectic nightlife so, even without the Bond connection, it would be a city worth visiting.

Hughes places their *fugu* meal not in Beppu but in Fukuoka where he writes that Fleming used a hot match end to show that the poison of the fish temporarily numbs the lips. An author's exaggeration as the edible flesh of the fish contains no poison at all but it makes for good story telling.

The detailed itinerary in Fukuoka is unknown. Fleming placed Shatterhand's castle and garden on a small promontory that stuck out from the rocky coastline. Reaching the fortress by land undetected was deemed impossible but it was believed that Bondo-san could enter via the seaward side by starting out from the small island of Kuro, home to a community of ama or pearl and abalone divers.

The promontory is not identified by name but geographically it is most likely to be Bishamonyama only a few miles west from Fukuoka and hence is the easy taxi ride that Fleming mentions. This is wooded and boasts a sharp summit rising to around 300 feet. Suffice to say that there is no castle here but the nearby island of Nokonoshima matches the size of Fleming's Kuro, and lies only about a kilometre off-shore. (Fleming says that Kuro is half a mile from the castle.)

Today Nokonoshima is celebrated as a particularly beautiful island but it has never been a place where *ama* lived. Indeed there is no *ama* island off Fukuoka and no island named Kuro.

Whether Fleming actually visited these locations we'll never know but it seems unlikely. Both could be easily seen from the city across the Hakata Bay so at least he could write something that was geographically correct.

They also visited the headquarters of the local police leaving the local police inspector more than bemused and confused by

Fleming's interrogation. This would later feature in the novel as Bond would be given a briefing by the police force in Fukuoka.

With their exploration over they caught an early evening Express back to Tokyo, one with an excellent dining car where they ate *sashimi, kabbayaki, sushi* while drinking (again) copious amounts of *sake*. (On his return to England, Fleming having found a taste for sake had some imported directly from Japan. He also brought back with him *wakame* seaweed.)

They arrived back late morning. On Fleming's last night in Tokyo, he, Hughes and Saito left the Okura and walked to the nearby American Club - a Tokyo institution since the late 1920s - for early evening drinks. After a cocktail, a loud discussion ensued with other journalists over the complicated way that sumo wrestlers wrap their *mawashi* (protective loin cloths) before the contest. Hughes thought this was a perverse preoccupation on the part of Fleming.

Suitably prepared, they took a taxi to the classic French restaurant the Prunier at the Marunouchi Kaikan where they ate full-bodied Hiroshima oysters and drank *sake*. (Hughes wrote that the reason the three men had not argued on their two week trip was because they had stuck to drinking *sake* - although Fleming was also partial to bourbon, which he argued was good for his heart.)

Hiroshima oysters are said to be the best in Japan and are particularly prized for their large fleshy nature; besides being eaten raw, they are fried, grilled, and used for tempura.

For a nightcap Hughes took Fleming to one of his old haunts, Ketel's in Ginza, a *bierkeller* and haunt of Nazi spies in the Second World War. At that time, the front entrance was shaped like a giant Bavarian beer barrel and the Nazis would drink *steins* of Japanese beer with their arms hugging the waspish waists of bar-girls. A piano had been draped with a large swastika flag.

It was here that the German-born communist spy Richard Sorge garnered secrets from drunken Nazis.

Hughes had a soft spot for Sorge, who was hanged in Tokyo's Sugamo prison on 7 November 1944 (and his body buried in Tama cemetery). Sorge worked for the Moscow government but having been captured by the Japanese, he was let down by Stalin who refused to do a deal with the Japanese for Sorge's release. (However in the same year that Fleming and Hughes were drinking in Ketels, the Russians made Sorge a Hero of the Soviet Union; his portrait appeared on a four kopeck stamp and a Moscow street was named after him.) Not that this information was new to Fleming: Sorge was well-known to Fleming and had already been mentioned in passing in *From Russia With Love*.

Hughes told Fleming that he had met and drank with the spy several times in the early 1940s - including a time when he stepped in and saved Sorge from a punch-up in Ketels. Hughes also ate with him in nearby Lohmeyers, where the anti-Nazi Germans would hang out. In fact Lohmeyers was older than Ketels as it was founded in 1921, and can still be found in Ginza at Nihonbashi where it serves authentic German dishes. Back when Fleming was in Tokyo, seven establishments served German food, accompanied by hearty accordion music to create an atmosphere of *Gemutlichkeit* - good-fellowship.

When Hughes worked in Tokyo during the early 1940s, Helmuth Ketel was still alive and Hughes described him as having a red corrugated face framed by white tangled hair and looked like a poor man's Beethoven. When Ketel was asked about his association with Sorge, he replied 'What would I know of espionage? I am just a poor pork butcher.'

How had Ketel come to be in Japan?

Helmuth Friedrich Carl Ernst Ketel was born on 25 April 1893 in Wedel. He volunteered for the German Navy and was sent in 1914 to Tsingtao, China. Here he was captured by Japanese forces, transferred to Japan and sent to the Narashino camp. In

December 1919 he was released but decided not to return to his homeland. He married a Japanese girl and in 1927 he opened Bar Rheingold and three years later, a restaurant called Ketels. Later the two establishments became one.

(Returning briefly to Richard Sorge: it is said that he met his Japanese wife Hanako Ishii in Rheingold where she worked as a hostess.)

However when Fleming visited, Ketel's was no longer quite such a sinister place, Helmuth had died in 1961 and his son Helmut had transformed the drinking den into a civilised restaurant serving typical German fare - wiener schnitzel, sausages and the such like - and with piped music by the likes of Elvis Presley and Pat Boone. This Fleming disliked, and he asked for it to be turned off while they ate pork knuckle with sauerkraut.

Hughes later wrote that unbeknown to him this was their last evening together. Their final meal was the following lunchtime, a *sayonara* banquet with members of Japan's secret police where Hughe's said they drank turtle blood, although Hughe's is slightly vague about the timing of this. He never saw Fleming again, and yet he thought in retrospect that Fleming was aware that he was slowly dying.

Hughes later wrote about the trip in an article for Saito's *This is Japan*. Appearing in the 1964 edition it was titled '*Sand in the Seaweed for James Bond*.' In 1972, his book '*Foreign Devil, Thirty Years of Reporting from the Far East*' was published by Deutsch with a chapter that covers his travels with Fleming and Saito, called *Sayonara* to James Bond. (Both have formed the reference point for this chapter.)

In January and February 1963, Fleming, as was his custom, returned to Goldeneye to write the novel. The first daft ran to 170 typed folio pages and thereafter it went through some minor corrections, written in the author's hand on the pages themselves.

Graham Thomas

The original manuscript is held at the Lilly Library, Indiana University, and it includes the following note from Fleming:

"I have visited Japan twice and, on the second occasion, as a conscientious biographer, I followed, as closely as prudence would allow, in the footsteps of James Bond. I was accompanied by the two expert investigators to whom this book is dedicated—one, the Far Eastern Representative of The Sunday Times, and the other the Editor-in-Chief of that distinguished annual 'This is Japan' published by the Asahi Shimbun. But, without these two friends at hand, and in my endeavour to do justice to the extremely foreign excitements and circumstances which James Bond will certainly have experienced, during the actual writing of this book I had very occasional recourse to four recent works of reference on Japan, all of which, for a closer understanding of the background to James Bond's perilous undertaking, I heartily recommend. They were:

Meeting with Japan by Fosco Maraini, Hutchinson 50/-

Hekura: The Diving Girls' Island by Fosco Maraini, Hamish Hamilton 25/-

The Heart of Japan by Alexander Campbell, Longmans 21/-

The Horned Islands by James Kirkup, Collins 35/-"

Fleming was sensitive to making mistakes in the book as in his previous book, *On Her Majesty's Secret Service*, he had inadvertently made errors that had been picked up by critics and experts alike. In a letter written to Michael Howard his publisher at Cape, he says that because of this he was being extra careful with his next book to ensure that no mistakes creep in and that 'we won't get Arthur Waley on our tail...'

(Waley was a distinguished and revered Orientalist and an acquaintance.)

Fleming also asked his friend Brian Hitch, a career diplomat who had spent several tours in Japan, for advice and Hitch ensured that Japanese spellings were correct and that the right names were used including that for the Japanese secret service (Fleming gives it the name *Koan-Chosa-Kyoku*). Does this organisation exist? Not exactly. The *Koan Chosacho* is the Public Safety Investigation Agency and is an investigative body looking at internal security only - an MI5 type body. Japan does not have a secret foreign intelligence service - or at least not formally, although there are rumours that one does now exist.

As he was finishing the book, Fleming once again wrote to William Plomer and reports that he has completed close to 65,000 words but still worries what the likes of Waley will have to say. Fleming continues, 'After all, when was it the last English novel about Japan was written? Just to give you an advance frisson, Bondo-san is about to pleasure Kissy Suzuki after she has stimulated his senses with toad sweat, a well-known Japanese aphrodisiac, as of course you know.' He also sent Plomer a copy of the manuscript and asked him to check it. Plomer told Fleming that Japanese words need to be italicised and Fleming worries that if this is the case there maybe too many and he knows that Michael Howard is not that keen on having too many in a book.

As to his comment regarding English language novels set in Japan, this is true. Very few had been written as most English language books were factual accounts of the writer's travels yet after the World War 2 some examples of fiction did emerge such as *The Hidden Flower* by Pearl S Buck, Vern Schneider's, *The Tea House*, and James Michener's *Sayonara*, all written in the early 1950s by American authors. In the later 1950s the British author Ronald Kirkbride wrote *Tamiko* - translated to the screen in a 1962 film starring Laurence Harvey who gets caught up with two girls in Tokyo, one American and the other Japanese.

But more likely Fleming wanted to write his Japan equivalent of Graham Greene's *Quiet American*. And, of course, it can be argued that Fleming was also influenced by the story of Cho-Cho-san, the spurned Japanese woman in the various versions of the

Madame Butterfly story itself based on *Madame Chrysanthème*, a novel by Pierre Loti,

At this point the American cryptographer Herbert Yardley makes a reappearance from Chapter 1.

To recap: he initial mission that James Bond is sent on at the start of *You Only Live Twice* is to negotiate with the Japanese secret service for access to their intelligence on the Russians. Fleming writes that the Japanese since the War have been building state-of-the-art decoding machines that have been cracking the most secret of Russian messages. However, for various political reasons, while they had been passing on this intelligence to the CIA, they had not been passing it to the British; nor was the CIA then passing it on to the British other than in a redacted summary.

Bond is sent to Japan to negotiate a swop: Japan's intelligence for British high-grade intelligence on China that was coming from a network within the country codenamed the Macau Blue Route.

Fleming called the Japanese cryptography machine MAGIC 44 and when Bond was meeting 'Tiger' Tanaka the Head of Japan's secret service, he was shown an example of the Russian intelligence that they had cracked with it.

So how does that relate to Herbert Yardley?

The only available evidence of any link between the two is that preface that Fleming wrote for Yardley's book on poker. There is no evidence that they ever met or corresponded but it would seem highly likely that Fleming would have read many of Yardley's books. Even *The Education of a Poker Player* was full of spy stories. And Fleming's background would mean that as a professional albeit desk-bound spy, he had knowledge of all of Yardley's shenanigans prior to and during the War.

But it is a reasonable conclusion that some of Yardley's knowledge and work (stuff that was not in the public realm at the time) and at least some of the stories he wrote about became a minor part of *You Only Live Twice* in one form or another.

Fleming of course was obsessive about getting his facts straight and so even if he deliberately mixed up the way he used names, he still wanted to ensure they were based on reality, and those in the know could nod knowingly if they read the novels.

Now back in Hong Kong, Hughes received a postcard from Fleming informing him of the novel's progress, the problems he was encountering, and wondering whether he needed to kill Bond off, 'Anyway he's had a good run which is more than most of us can say. Everything seems a lot of trouble these days - too much trouble. Keep alive.'

Here was Fleming acknowledging that he faced death. The descent of Bond into his own depression and his persistent drinking sadly reflected all too closely aspects of Flemings own life, and without doubt, the story has a stream of despondent self-analysis and reflection running through it. And at the end of the book, in one sense, Bond does indeed die.

Hughes, it should be said, was cross at Fleming's morbidity and wrote back saying that if Fleming sent another letter like this, he would refuse to reply.

By April 1963 Fleming's typist, Jean Frampton had produced eight copies for distribution to the editorial staff at Cape and within days he had received the most enthusiastic letter from Michael Howard his publisher. Howard thought that Fleming had broken away from his usual formula and that this was a good thing; he applauded the lack of branded goods (but wondered if this was because Fleming wanted to discourage imports of Japanese products), and was congratulatory on how this was a brilliant diversion 'after the Tracy episode.' Furthermore, he had no issue with the detailed descriptions of Japanese life and culture as he thought these would make unfamiliar but fascinating reading for Bond fans.

This was a huge reassurance to Fleming who confessed that perhaps he had written too much of a travelogue and that the action was being introduced too late. (In one early printing, it started on page 170 of 240 pages.)

The typescript was corrected over the period March to May 1963. One extant copy has extensive corrections and proof markings made by a copy-editor in purple ballpoint. This was then sent to Fleming to be checked and agreed. His own comments were made in blue ballpoint and he made revisions to around 65 pages, mostly single words or short phrases but including one eight-line textual addition towards the end of the book. The manuscript then went through further revisions across a number of months before proofing of the book commenced towards the end of 1963 with 500 copies printed. One bookseller described one of the proofs as having mainly (and numerous) typographical mistakes, which were corrected. The preface was missing, and the verso of the half title had the title as 'On Her Mjsty's Scrt Srvic[]'. The copyright page lacked both the publisher's address and the papermaker and binder's credit, and the chapter 'Magic 44' appears in square caps.

The issuing of the proof coincided with a discussion about whether Fleming should use the word '*tanka*' or '*haiku*.' In a terse letter, Fleming writes in frustration 'we seem to be having the most tremendous argument about what is a '*tanka*' and what is '*haiku*' and I can't understand why someone can't look it up in a dictionary and find the correct answer.'

In the end, the answer was indeed found: both are short-form poetry and have a relationship with one another but '*tanka*' is slightly longer, with five lines and usually 32 syllables, and '*haiku*' is shorter still, with three lines and 17 syllables.

Derived from the style of the poet Basho, a *haiku* was composed to accompany the book's title. Hughes in his book writes that he thought the first version that Fleming wrote was the best:

You only live twice:

Once when you are born,

And once when you are about to die.

RICHARD HUGHES

Thwack!

Bond has snatched Dikko Henderson's walking stick and hit him hard with it across the leg.

'I'm glad you got it right.' says Henderson, 'I lost that in Singapore in '42. Oh, you must excuse this rather odd mixture of styles, but I refuse to go entirely Japanese. Very fond of some of these old things... You've never been to Japan before, have you?'

A minute later, Henderson is dead, killed by an assassin who has knifed him in the back through a shoji screen.

Henderson's screen time in the film version of *You Only Live Twice* is brief, leaving little opportunity for Charles Gray to develop the character. What we do see is a rather languid, off-hand persona, who never returned home after the War, and is now somewhat dismissive of Bond, the newcomer.

But even this briefest of appearances bears no relation to the Dikko Henderson in the novel. Henderson is Australia's secret service chief in Tokyo, and is afforded a greater piece of the action as he introduces Bond to Japan. The nature of the man is clearly set out: a loud, hard drinking, whoring Australian who leaves a trail of empty whiskey and brandy bottles behind him, looking and speaking like an ex-prize fighter who has long taken to drink. He speaks fluent Japanese, intimately understands

Japan's way of life, is rather dismissive of the Japanese as a race, claims that Tokyo is a bloody awful place to live, and has what we might term an old fashioned view of a woman's position in society. In short, he was portrayed as a typical ex-pat or Old Asia Hand of the period. 'What's a girl's bottom for anyway,' he remarks when Bond points out that the night before he had slapped a girl so hard on the bottom that she fell over.

Our literary Henderson does not wear an artificial limb, and is not assassinated. In fact he bows out of the story discreetly, remarking to Bond, 'you're on your own now.'

It will be widely known by Bond aficionados that Dikko Henderson was based on Fleming's friend Richard Hughes, an Australian journalist, and a larger-than-life character who had been working as a journalist in Asia since the 1940s.

So who was this Richard Hughes in real life? Was he, in any way, like Dikko Henderson? The bare facts in themselves suggest an interesting man.

Born Richard Joseph Hughes in Melbourne in 1906, he died in Hong Kong in 1984 having spent most of his working life in Asia as a highly regarded journalist, writing for publications such as *The Times*, *The Economist*, the *Far Eastern Economic Review* the *New York Times*, and various Australian newspapers. Along the way he married three times, and was awarded the CBE.

He was one of four siblings and the eldest child of Richard Hughes and Katie, née McGlade. Hughes Snr. was a sometime furniture salesman but also a popular and celebrated Melbourne ventriloquist. Little is known of his paternal forebears other than they hailed from Wales and were Baptists, and apparently the family were none too happy when the Protestant Hughes married the Catholic McGlade - whose family were originally Irish farmers.

However the marriage was a success, and Richard Hughes Senior established himself as a leading ventriloquist. He wrote at least two books on the subject, the first being *Ventriloquism Ancient and Modern*, and in 1902 he authored *How To Become A Ventriloquist (Art Of Voice Throwing)*. (His trusty sidekick by the way was Tommy Squarehead.) However, some years later he gave up show business because his wife Katie, as a strict Catholic and, by some accounts, a domineering woman, objected. Thereafter Hughes Snr. would sometimes confess that he thought he had failed in life by giving up what he thought would have been a lucrative career.

Hughes Junior clearly inherited his father's humour, oratorial skills, stage presence and, relevant for later in his life, a love of reading and in particular, the Sherlock Holmes stories. Tall, solidly built, and imposing, Hughes Jnr. was later described by the journalist Pat Burgess as `fleshy and pale with a big head and a noble dome with thinning silver hair'. Robert M. Shaplen, once a Hong Kong-based Far East correspondent, said that Hughes was a big, robust man with a dry wit, 'a terrific storyteller, a raconteur with a raconteur's big laugh, a tremendous fund of knowledge and an incredible memory.' Fellow journalists variously described him as gregarious, generous but also complex, and someone who wanted to be in control and the centre of attention. In his younger days, Hughes was an amateur boxer.

After a peripatetic start to his career - when Hughes variously worked as a poster artist, a railway shunter, and in public relations - he moved into journalism in 1934 working for the *Melbourne Star* before moving to Sydney to work on the *Telegraph* papers.

By this time, his first wife had committed suicide by cyanide poisoning, and the widowed Hughes decided when leaving Melbourne that his own son Richard be left behind and raised by Hughes' parents. (That's right: there was Richard Hughes Snr, Richard Hughes Jnr, and Baby Richard Hughes.)

His qualities as a journalist were soon recognised and, by 1939, he had been promoted to principal assignment editor for both

Telegraph papers. A year later in 1940, he travelled briefly to Japan for the first time. He paid his own way by taking long service leave to do this as he held the belief that Asia and Japan were part of the future for Australia and he wanted to be where the action was.

He settled in Tokyo's Imperial Hotel and began to trawl the city for contacts. One of these was Richard Sorge who was then Head of the Soviet spy ring in Asia but who was most likely a double agent also working the Nazi government. Hughes described him as the greatest spy of all times.

This ability to quickly identify key contacts was typically Hughes. Someone who was adept at quickly assessing a situation and sniffing out stories, and soon he was sending dispatches back to the *Telegraph* many of which centred on his increasing belief that Japan was edging towards war and was not in fact looking for any trade partnerships with Australia. He also rapidly concluded that the Australian Government needed to be better prepared in case of war and drop their complacent attitude that Japan would never be better equipped and prepared than the West. In one article for example he summed up Japan's Armed forces as: Navy – Powerful; Army – tough but weak in mechanised forces; Airforce – poor and also air raid defenses also very weak. It was almost as if he was being a very public spy.

By the time Japan did go to war, Hughes was safely back in Sydney – but not for long. In 1943 he was assigned as a war correspondent to North Africa but this was unexpectedly short-lived as he had to be shipped home after developing severe rheumatic fever in Cairo.

After the War he returned to Japan to cover the occupation. However for one reason or another his rather short-sighted employers back in Sydney decided they no longer needed a full time foreign correspondent in Tokyo and, after a couple of years, summoned him back. Instead he resigned, took up freelancing and also had a stint as the manager of the Foreign Correspondents' Club. In his memoir, *Foreign Devil*, Hughes would later describe the FCC as a 'makeshift bordello, inefficient gaming-house and blackmarket centre.'

At the same time as Hughes was in Tokyo, Fleming had joined the Kemsley newspaper group as Foreign Manager. Here he set up the Imperial and Foreign Service, a global network of foreign correspondents. It was quickly nicknamed Mercury – its cable address – and provided articles across all the Kemsley newspapers. Many years later it became known that it provided cover for more than one British secret service agent. For example Antony Terry, the *Sunday Times* reporter in Bonn, doubled as an intelligence officer in Vienna and Berlin. Fleming despatched Cedric Salter of SOE to Barcelona, Ian Colvin (close links to the Secret Intelligence Service) to Berlin, and Henry Brandon, an agent to Washington. Donald McCormick, formerly of Naval Intelligence, became Fleming's stringer in Tangier. In fact in his office, Fleming had a large map on the wall dotted with coloured pins showing the locations of all the correspondents he was running. If nothing else, and Fleming was never explicit about its dual purpose, it was an informal network of spies that could be called upon to deliver incidental intelligence.

Around 1948 (the date is not known precisely) Hughes was taken on as Fleming's man in Japan – although he continued to write despatches for a variety of publications, was also on a retainer for his ex-employers in Sydney, and would also lecture at the Royal Institute of International Affairs Far Eastern Group on developments in Japan.

In February 1956 he achieved a major scoop when he obtained an all but exclusive interview in Moscow with the Soviet spies Donald Maclean and Guy Burgess, the two great Soviet moles within the British establishments. On the verge of being arrested these two had defected to the Soviet Union and then disappeared. It was Fleming who had sent Hughes to Moscow to gain one of the first interviews with Nikita Khrushchev ahead of his first state visit to the U.K. This failed to materialise and he was about to fly out when he was called by telephone to go to Room 101 in the Hotel National where he and a Reuters man had the briefest of interviews with the two traitors. This rediscovery set London buzzing and, as Hughes later said, it was possibly his biggest story ever before admitting that, 'most good stories depend on a pressman being in the right place at the right time and that was me with this story.'

Diplomatic Mystery Ends

Burgess and Maclean Tell All

Moscow. Sunday: Last night I met with Donald Maclean and Guy Burgess in the Hotel National overlooking the Red Square and Hotel National. Thus ended four and half years of mystery and doubt of their whereabouts...

It was after Moscow that Hughes moved to Hong Kong, as he perceived - correctly - that in the future China would become of greater global interest. Here he would remain until his death.

Hughes was appointed CBE in 1980, He wrote several books, including *The Chinese Communes* (1960), *Hong Kong: Borrowed Place, Borrowed Time* (1968), and his autobiographical *Foreign Devil* (1972). And not only did he appear in *You Only Live Twice* but he was also the inspiration for 'Old Craw' the Hong Kong in John le Carré's *The Honourable Schoolboy*. le Carré had met Hughes when visiting the colony, and later described him as 'a kind of journalistic Eiffel Tower.' Hughes was famous: he appeared on the *Michael Parkinson Show*, and was introduced as 'the doyen of that most glamorous breed of journalists, the Foreign Correspondent' and he also was a subject of the Australian version of *This Is Your Life*.

Hughes had been portrayed in two novels as a spy. Did that reflect the reality in his own life? Well it was his son revealed that his father had been a double agent for MI6 and the KGB.

It was said that the Russians at a Tokyo cocktail party had recruited Hughes in 1951, although this was not unusual as most competent journalists in Asia were approached by such organisations during the Cold War and, as noted earlier, it might well have been the case that Fleming's foreign correspondents were feeding information back to London. Indeed, *The Times'* archive on Fleming, strongly suggests that Fleming's own network of foreign correspondents was a *de facto* spy ring working on the side for MI6.

It has been claimed that Hughes told Fleming that the KGB had made overtures to recruit him. Fleming consulted British Intelligence who then told Hughes to accept the offer. British Intelligence provided Hughes with false information to feed the Russians.

This aspect of Hughes' life has been much reported on, with the added spice more recently that he set up his own network of informants under the guise of a Tokyo-based Sherlock Holmes appreciation society called the Baritsu Chapter.

We know that along with twenty-five others, Hughes was a founder member in 1948. These included the then Japanese Prime Minister, other leading foreign journalists, and members of the Japanese establishment and literati. (Hughes wrote an article for *The Sunday Times*, published February 26, 1950 that explained the setting up of the chapter in Tokyo but noting its absence in Russia, 'The philosophic observer may well speculate on the significance in current international affairs of the continued absence of any branch of the Baker Street Irregulars in Moscow and of the stubborn refusal of Joseph Stalin to read any of the Sherlock Holmes adventures.')

However, in a paper written by Ian Wilson for the *Australian Journal of Communication*, it is concluded that while it was possible that Hughes did work as a spy this is only through inference and the case, even if highly likely, is unproven. Hughes never once admitted it publicly and within his collected papers kept at the National Library of Australia there is, as Wilson writes, no smoking gun. Wilson also concludes from his research that even if he was working with British Intelligence through Fleming, they in fact decided that Hughes should not be a double agent and told him to decline the Russian's offer.

On the other hand his biographer Norman Macswan is convinced Hughes was acting as a double agent but was unable to include this information in *The Man Who Read The East Wind* because Hughes placed an embargo on it.

These stories perhaps place too much emphasis on Hughes as spy in the James Bond mold. British Intelligence was not alone in using journalists as a source of information that would be fed back to the intelligence officers in the embassies. Any good pressman would have a range of contacts and Hughes' despatches were renowned for their depth and insight. However these officers would also use intelligence gathered by local operatives in the field, by British companies (who might well have their own intelligence network), and British businessmen working in the country; in other words a veritable network was used and the term spy should only be used in the most generic sense.

The idea that Hughes was a double agent is definitely open to question if not great doubt. Hughes was not at the heart of the Establishment, and he was not privy to intelligence secrets in the Burgess and Maclean mold. The Russians would know this of course, and would have been surprised and suspicious if he suddenly started passing on information that clearly a journalist would be unaware of. Likewise, what information would he get from the Russians that would be useful to the British?

We should also discount the idea that the Baritsu Chapter was set up as a spy network: the Japanese Prime Minister would attend a meeting to spill secrets? Beyond unlikely. In any case

Hughes was a co-founder and while a leading light was not the only one responsible for its continued existence. And as we saw earlier with the setting up of Alcoholics Synonymous, he had a penchant for setting up clubs.

As Fleming highlights in *You Only Live Twice*, it was the Americans who were the prime intelligence gatherers not only in Japan but across Asia, and the British largely relied on the Americans passing on relevant information. In fact, as noted earlier, the reason Bond is despatched to Japan is to try and persuade the Japanese to give the British intelligence that the US are withholding.

In the end it doesn't matter if Hughes was a spy or not as the man generated enough remarkable stories to fill a library of books and, as his son once said about his father, 'he was a man of mystery, and it was a role he relished.'

TORAO SAITO

The dedication in *You Only Live Twice* reads, 'TO Richard Hughes and Torao Saito BUT FOR WHOM ETC....'

Both Hughes and Saito had now been metamorphosed into characters in the novel: Hughes became Richard Lovelace 'Dikko' Henderson, ostensibly of HM's Australian Diplomatic Corps but in truth a spy for Australia's Secret Service in Tokyo while Saito had become 'Tiger' Tanaka, head of the Japanese Secret Service

Tanaka takes a pivotal role and is a presence throughout the novel. Bond meets him first in Tokyo to negotiate a deal between the British and Japanese secret services; and then, after Tanaka insists that for the deal to go through Bond needs to assassinate Blofeld aka Dr. Shatterhand, he accompanies Bond through much of the mission.

It is generally accepted that the Henderson character - at least reasonably if not closely - matched the real life Hughes. Hughes published his memoirs, a biography was written and, as a larger than life character, much is known about the man. And despite Hughes' blustering over Fleming's lampooning, it is likely that he was rather pleased with his portrayal. On the other hand, less is known about Saito, and so the opportunity to compare the fictional Tanaka with the real life Saito is a little diminished.

In the novel, Tanaka is described as having a big creased brown face with a wide smile but a face that could suddenly flick to the look of a cruel samurai. We know he enjoyed sake, Suntory whisky, and that he spoke impeccable English. His age is not stated explicitly but he is in early sixties when he meets Bond, and close to retirement.

He was highly educated having taken a First in PPE at Trinity, Cambridge, had a firm understanding of the West, a Black Belt at judo, and was a spy in the Japanese Embassy in London during the 1930s. On Japan's entry into the Second World War, he was appointed as the personal aide to Admiral Onishi then Chief of Staff for the 11 Air Fleet, and who later was responsible for setting up the kamikaze units. As Japan's fortunes deteriorated, Tanaka volunteered and was training as a kamikaze pilot just as the War ended. His age was nearly forty. Of his reasoning for participating in the War Tanaka said, 'I plead youth and the heat of a war that I thought would bring much glory to my country. I was mistaken.'

Just as Bond had Universal Exports, Tanaka's cover was the Bureau of All Asia Folkways, producing literature that was offered for free to foreigners such as, according to Tanaka, the Americans, Swiss and Germans. Later, with obvious distaste, Tanaka goes on at length about the Americanisation of Japan– the *Scuola di Coca Cola* he calls it. It is clearly a subject that angers him but in the end he apologies to Bond and says he was 'letting off steam.'

As Hughes was a close friend, Fleming undoubtedly felt he could be free and yet honest with his fictional characterisation of Hughes. It is probable that he was more respectful in approaching the fictionalisation of Saito, who had become a friend only through Hughes' introduction and, of course, Fleming would be more than aware of the formal way that the Japanese approach friendships. As a consequence, Fleming was less likely to take liberties.

So who was the real Torao Saito?

Torao Saito was born in Tokyo in 1902 at a time when Japan was going through a period of radical modernisation and westernisation. The early 20 century was also the time when Japan flexed its military muscles and, in 1910, had annexed Korea.

In the 1920s Saito attended Waseda University, one of the most prestigious in the country, and graduated from its Department of Architecture in 1930.

It is this same year that the first accessible and tangible record crops up: an inscribed book that comes from Saito's library. The book *Wie Baut Amerika* was written by the celebrated architect Richard Neutra – Austrian born but by 1930 living and practicing in the US.

"With much appreciation for the fine reception in Tokyo. Dedicated to Mr. T. Saitô Richard Neutra June 10th 1930"

Neutra had visited Japan that year and given talks in Tokyo and Osaka. It is a matter of record that a small reception had been held in the Asakusa district of Tokyo, and perhaps it was this reception that Saito had organised so well.

Rather than working as a full-time architect after graduation, he joined instead the Asahi Newspaper Co. first as a science reporter and then as an aviation correspondent. Asahi was then - and still is - one of the oldest and largest of Japan's national newspaper and magazine groups, and generally thought to hold liberal views. However this period also coincided with Japan invading Manchuria and becoming increasingly right wing and nationalistic, with the government progressively dominated by the military.

While working at Asahi, the Second Sino-Japanese War broke out in 1937 and, for a period of time, Saito was sent to the Shanghai office, which was the biggest foreign newspaper Bureau in the city. However by the time Japan attacked Pearl Harbour at the end of 1941, Saito had been promoted to editing Asahi's monthly magazine *Koku Asahi* (Aviation Asahi) having launched it at the beginning of 1941. It's role simply was to expound on the greatness and superiority of the Japanese air force, explain in depth an understanding of foreign fighting craft and, as the Second World war progressed, publish the numbers and types of enemy aircraft that had been shot down.

In 1942, Saito was despatched to Java as part of a team to examine American Flying Fortress warplanes that had been abandoned as the Japanese invaded the island. The Japanese were adept at evaluating American aircraft design and using the best bits to develop their own aircraft.

After his visit, Saito wrote in the *Koku Asahi*, 'the maintenance facilities for the B-17 in Java were excellent for that time and existing conditions. It appeared that Bandung Field was the maintenance base for the Americans, and it was here that our technicians from the *Giken* performed their initial flight evaluation tests on these newest of American war birds.'

In 1943, Asahi published a book that Saito edited, using many of his photographs of captured Allied planes, called *Anatomy of the Enemy's Aircraft*.

(It would seem that *Koku Asahi* was highly successful and continued to be printed through to the final month of Japan's defeat even though paper and ink supplies were in short supply due to damage caused by air raids and when most other aviation magazines had been discontinued.)

At some stage, he also became a war correspondent attached to the Imperial Navy as evidenced for example by the piece he wrote for the *Syonan Shimbun* seen on the preceding page.

Many years later, the Australian war correspondent Denis Warner wrote in the *New York Times*,

'Torao Saito, a noted Japanese war correspondent, and later a close friend, used to claim that his home, a long way from the Nakajima aircraft factory, had been destroyed and that I was responsible!'

After the War, Saito continued to be employed by the Asahi newspaper group including taking on the editorship of the monthly *Kagaku Asahi* (Scientific Asahi), a leading science magazine that made general science popular throughout Japan.

According to Hughes, it was during the Occupation that he and Saito became friends when they met at the Asahi offices in late 1945.

Three years later in 1948, Hughes and a group of like-minded people decided that there ought to be a branch of the Sherlock Holmes fan club, the Baker Street Irregulars, in Japan, and so they started one, naming it The Baritsu Chapter. Saito was one of the first members.

By 1953, Saito had been appointed as chief editor of *This Is Japan*, a lavishly illustrated, large format journal published annually. Running to over three hundred pages and printed in both colour as well as black and white, this featured articles authored by Japanese and foreign experts on many aspects of the country: its culture and arts, the sciences, manufacturing, and every day life. The annual was distributed free to embassies and foreign businesses in Japan, and overseas through the Japanese embassies to governments, academics, and institutes of education. Hughes wrote an article for the first edition entitled *The Vanishing Occupation*, one called *So You Understand the Japanese* in the second edition of 1955, and the next year an article on the islands of Japan, when it was noted that he was a foreign correspondent for the Kemsley Newspaper Group, and the *Economist*. Over the years, Saito was able to persuade a great number of distinguished people to contribute including a plethora of Japanese and foreign writers, artists, actors, filmmakers, diplomats and politicians and, from abroad, diplomats journalists. Ultimately, Fleming was among them.

Did this mean that he had dropped the practice of architecture all together? Apparently not. The large number of houses destroyed in the Second World War gave Japan a new, if rather unfortunate opportunity to rebuild and to develop housing design. In 1958 Saito was joint editor of a book called *Japanese Houses Today*. Inside it stated that he had been an architect of many houses in Japan and examples of his work were included.

It was in 1959 that he first met and befriended Fleming when he accompanied Fleming and Hughes on the former's first visit to Tokyo.

Fleming was later to described Saito thus:

'He was a chunky reserved man with considerable stores of quiet humour and intelligence, and with a subdued but rather tense personality. He looked like a fighter – one of those warlords of the Japanese films. He had, in fact, been a judo black belt, one rank below the red-belt elite, and there was a formidable quality about him that I enjoyed.'

Following this trip, Fleming wrote an article that appeared in the 1961 edition of *This is Japan* called *Spy Writers Reconnaissance in Japan*, which is very much the same as the chapter on Tokyo in *Thrilling Cities*.

As described in the preceding chapter, one year later Saito joined Hughes and Fleming again, and while Hughes says that both he and Saito drew up the itinerary for their fourteen day trip, it is clear that Saito was responsible for all the detailed arrangements.

It was also in 1962 that Saito attended and lectured at the 55th Annual Assembly of the Royal Architectural Institute of Canada, which is where the portrait of him was taken.

As touched on previously, in *You Only Live Twice* Tiger complains about the *Scuola di Coca Cola* – the takeover of Japan by American culture. Interestingly in the 1964 edition of *This is Japan*, Saito assembled seven famous writers to compose a re-

The Definitive Story Of You Only Live Twice

quiem to 'lost Tokyo.' One of them, Masajiro Kojima, wrote, 'The Japanese who are so fond of abandoning what is their own, once took a fancy to building exact replicas of Chinese towns. This time it seems they are abandoning their own traditions in order to build the perfect American town.' It would seem that Fleming was only capturing Saito's strongly held beliefs.

Saito's last edition of *This is Japan* as editor was in 1966 after which he retired but remained as an editorial advisor for the 1967 edition. Richard Hughes continued to write for *This is Japan* until it was folded with the 1971 edition. In his final piece he wrote,

'*This is Japan* was a damned good publication. In its field, I know none better. It was put on the road, lonely, cocky and enquiring, by a small skeleton team of old Asahi pros – old in experience but not in years – under the direction of 'Tiger' Saito.

'Tiger' was an editor and administrator of drive, imagination and manifold talents. He delegated authority with aplomb and assurance. He was himself both a newspaper reporter and a photographer of distinction. He was also an architect and an airman and he brought therefore a sense of design and harmony and a predilection for wide horizons to his editorial planning and thinking. Any pressman who worked with him became a better pressman. Tiger is my oldest Japanese friend...'

Saito died on 24 February 1971, and an obituary was published in the May edition of the Japanese architectural magazine, *Kenchiku Zasshi*. In Hughes' memoir published a year later in 1972, he refers to Saito as his 'late friend.'

Hughes also roguishly complained that like himself, Saito had been shamefully lampooned in *You Only Live Twice*. He might have also mentioned that Fleming could not resist writing at least one gentle joke at Saito's expense: Bond is staying on the *ama* island where he marries Kissy. He is shown the toilet, a 'little shack with the hole in the ground and the neatly quartered

Graham Thomas

pages of the *Asahi Shimbun* on a nail.'

XAVIER KOIKE

Fleming dedicated a copy of *You Only Live Twice* to Xavier Koike (1922 -1999) the son of Ken Koike a Japanese dentist who practiced in London off the Tottenham Court Road, and May Samuels his English mother. It would appear that the family moved to Japan in the 1930s and when War broke out like all suspicious foreign nationals he was detained and imprisoned. Following Japan's surrender he was released and acted as a translator during the trials of suspected Japanese war criminals. Later he worked for the Supreme Court, helping to oversee the administration of Japan under the American occupation.

During the 1970s, records show he was living back in London in Sussex Mews, London W2. He had married and had several children. However he died in Yokohama, Japan in 1999.

At some stage he connected with Fleming, and the two would write to each other. According to on-line information from a bookseller, Koike's family said that he provided Fleming with information regarding Japan's administrative processes and agencies, as well as ideas for locations in Japan that could be used in *You Only Live Twice*.

While it has not been possible to independently verify this information on the other hand there is no reason to doubt the story.

BOND

In March 1964, some eighteen months after his visit, *You Only Live Twice* was published in the UK, the twelfth novel in the James Bond series, and whose total worldwide sales had now exceeded seventeen million.

The cover was designed and painted by the artist Richard Chopping - for which he was paid £315 - and features a toad, dragonfly and a pink chrysanthemum. (Chopping was responsible for nine of the Bond covers.) He lived in Wivenhoe, Essex and as he wanted to draw the toad from life, he visited nearby Colchester Natural History Museum to see if they kept a specimen.

The price for the hardback was 16s.

In Japan, it was published under the name 007は二度死ぬ by the publisher Hayakawa Shobo and translated by Kazuo Inoue 井上一夫.

A month later, an abridged version of the novel was serialised in *Playboy* in three parts across April, May and June for which Fleming was paid $35,000. (Fleming had first met Ray Russell, the Executive Editor of *Playboy*, on a visit to Chicago in 1959; the two had remained in contact ever since with serialisations of the novels starting with the cinematic release of *Dr No*. At one time, Fleming told Russell that he should open an office in England as *Playboy* was becoming increasingly popular.)

At the same time a serialised version also appeared in the *Daily Express*.

In the novel, Richard Hughes becomes the Australian spy Dikko Henderson (as per the signed copy of the novel seen at the start of the chapter) and Tiger Saito became Tiger Tanaka, boss of the Japanese intelligence service. The storyline features, of course, many of the places that Fleming had visited and follows the same journey down to Kyushu. Indeed, one of the critics' criticisms of the book was, as Fleming had feared, that it was more travel book than spy novel even if it had captured Japanese culture particularly well. *The Times* erred on the harsh side, saying that Fleming had largely populated Japan with geisha girls, bath girls and cabaret girls 'with their tummies tucked in' and it was clear that Fleming was tiring of Bond.

In the preceding novel, *On Her Majesty's Secret Service*, the head of SPECTRE, Ernst Blofeld, instigates the murder of Bond's newly-wed wife Tracy Bond. The storyline continues *In You Only Live Twice* where we find that this loss has led to Bond slipping into an alcoholic depression and his work and attitude deteriorate to the extent that the secret service decide that perhaps they need to sack him. However, as highlighted in the previous chapter, he is handed one last chance to redeem himself and sent to Japan on a mission to convince the head of Japan's secret intelligence service, Tiger Tanaka, to provide Britain with information from radio transmissions captured from the Soviet Union. In exchange, London will allow the Japanese access to one of their own sources, information from the Macau Blue Route network working in China.

The real-life background to this was the poor state of the UK in world affairs, an issue that troubled Fleming. The British secret service had found itself distrusted, particularly in the US because of the defections of four of Britain's top spies to the Soviet Union and the unravelling Profumo Affair where a Government cabinet minister had an affair with Christine Keeler, a high-class call-girl - who simultaneously also happened to be courting a Russian spy. All this led to the US mistrusting the British and withholding secrets.

However, when Bond meets Tiger Tanaka, he is not only browbeaten about Britain's lamentable security lapses but also on her less than influential role in global affairs. This was another Fleming bugbear. He had seen his adopted country Jamaica become independent in 1962, and to him the erosion of the British Empire was yet another symbol of Britain's decline.

When Bond's makes his offer to Tanaka to swop intelligence Tanaka further tells Bond that they have already penetrated Britain's Blue Route intelligence network, leaving Bond with nothing to bargain with.

Instead, Tanaka asks Bond to kill Dr. Guntram Shatterhand, who operates a politically embarrassing 'Garden of Death' in a rebuilt ancient castle on the island of Kyushu. This, he has populated, with all manner of poisonous plants, and deadly animals such as poisonous snakes, and piranha. (All these he needed to import, as Japan has almost no indigenous poisonous plants and animals.) To his Government's anger, people were flocking to the garden to commit suicide but Shatterhand proclaimed all innocence and indeed blamed the authorities for not stopping the would-be suicides before they entered his property. To have Shatterhand killed by an outsider would be politically expedient.

On examining photos of Shatterhand and his wife, Bond immediately recognises them as Tracy's murderers, Ernst Stavro Blofeld and Irma Bunt. Bond accepts the mission, now one of revenge, but without divulging their true identities as he believes that if he did, the US, Japanese and British governments would step in officially and take the mission away.

Tanaka tells him that to succeed he must become Japanese. He must become Bondo-san. Using cosmetics he is made to look

The Definitive Story Of You Only Live Twice

Japanese, after which he and Tanaka take a slow journey from Tokyo to Kyushu so that Bondo-san has the time to learn to think and act like a native. This idea may have had its genesis with his editor at Cape, William Plomer who, as was noted in the last chapter, had written in his autobiography that he had found in the 1920s that to live successfully in Japan he had to leave his former life behind and adopt the ways of the Japanese.

On arrival at an island close to Blofeld's fortress in Fukuoka, Bondo-san is helped by former Japanese film star Kissy Suzuki - and now an *ama* - to find a way into Blofeld's garden.

While he is successful initially, and sees first hand the terrible suicides taking place, Bondo-san is captured and Bunt identifies him as the British secret agent and not a deaf mute Japanese coal miner. After surviving excruciating interrogation, Bondo-san kills Blofeld and then destroys the fortress killing Bunt. Upon escaping, he suffers a head injury which, added to his other injuries, leaves him without memory and happy to believe that he can live as a Japanese fisherman with Kissy.

When Bondo-san's health improves, Kissy ensures that he does not find out his true identity nor that he is discovered by the authorities. After the administration of an aphrodisiac and the sharing of a Pillow Book, Kissy and Bond make love and she becomes pregnant. However she keeps this to herself. There comes a time when Bond has some glimmer of memory of times past that tells him that he must rediscover this past, and for this he must travel to Russia leaving Kissy behind.

So ends the story.

What follows here is an exploration of the key Japanese details that are found in the novel. This also fills in gaps in the knowledge of Fleming's own trip.

The time when the novel is set is not made explicit but Fleming wrote in a contemporaneous style. Bond also makes a passing mention of the Olympics so it can be reasonably assumed that the setting is encompasses 1962 and 1963.

The novel opens with Bond attending a *geisha* party with Tiger Tanaka, one that obviously reflected Fleming's own experience when researching the novel. Tiger smokes Dunhill cigarettes while Bond plays games with the *geisha*, drinks copious amounts of *sake* despite being warned that it is not a drink to be underestimated. He ignores this for the rest of the novel as, at every opportunity, he is seen to drink hot *sake* by the flask.

Should *sake* be drunk hot or cold? Is the correct temperature 98.4 degrees? Nowadays the answer is yes to both hot and cold, although the precise temperature is not an issue as different *sakes* can be drunk warm, warmer and hot.

But back when Fleming visited Japan, more often *sake* was drunk hot for the simple fact that its quality had certainly deteriorated after the War, and a rougher grade of *sake* was the norm. In fact *sake* was generally drunk hot even before the Second World War not least as hot *sake* was a useful drink in the winter because of Japan's unheated draughty and extremely cold homes. Nowadays, a significantly higher quality of *sake* is brewed, the variety and the subtly of taste is immense, and it would be a sacrilege to heat it up - as bad as drinking hot Chablis. Instead, high quality *sake* should be drunk slightly chilled - but not too cold otherwise the taste will be lost.

And is *sake* strong? Not as strong as suggested in the novel as its alcohol content is around 17 degrees proof, similar to a sherry or slightly higher than the strongest wines. *Sake* is often called a rice wine but this is incorrect: it is more beer-like in the brewing process but more accurately it is a unique process in its own right. Polished rice kernels (and the degree of polish affects the nature of the end product) have a mould (*koji-kin*) added to them which converts the starch into sugars. In turn, yeasts from the *koji* turns the sugars into alcohol. Water is added and the whole mash is allowed to sit for about a month and then is pressed, strained, blended and bottled. And like beer, it is a beverage that should be drunk within a few months of being brewed. It is the nature and quality of the four simple ingredients of rice, *koji* and water that fundamentally affects the final product. (Without forgetting that around 100 different rice strains are used today.)

During the party Bond is asked to compose a *tanka* by the girls. Of course his thoughts also turn to wondering if he might be able to lure one of the girls to bed but Tiger observes that he won't be much of a bed companion for the girl. This brings us to another often confusing myth about Japan: were *geisha* prostitutes? First and foremost they were highly skilled entertainers who underwent years of training. When they emerged as a entity in the Edo period, they performed in teahouses located in the pleasure quarter of Japan's cities, the area where all manner of entertainment was available including prostitution. In the early days there may have been a blurring of roles and it is certainly true that *geisha* might become long-term companions, possibly courtesans to their wealthy customers but they are emphatically not prostitutes but skilled performers who never stop learning their art. Yes, their skill is to make men feel superior and funny and clever; and their chatter can sometimes be downright naughty but they are not there to jump into bed with.

When he played one of Japan's favourite games, Scissors Paper Stone (*janken*), Bond beat Tiger. Bond says in reference to the upcoming Tokyo Olympics that he must get the game adopted by the Olympics so that he can represent Great Britain.

Afterwards, they retire to Tiger's house outside Tokyo - and closer to Yokohama as they could see the lights and smell the harbour and sea. Yokohama was also where Tiger's office was located with its nightingale floor of the type that Fleming had seen in Kyoto. Why Fleming has made Yokohama the location is unknown as he had not visited Yokohama previously but perhaps he wanted to show a tranquil restful side to Tokyo and one which more suited the Oxford-educated Tanaka.

The story then switches back in time and recounts the reasons Bond had been sent to Japan, his arrival and his initial meetings with Tiger.

Bond had flown to Japan on a JAL Douglas DC-8 named *Yoshino* - a real name that had been given to one of JAL's first jets - from London Airport on a route that went west over the Artic - rather than east as it does today. (At the time, the west route was fastest.) Before departure the stewardess bowed and handed him a fan, a hot-towel and, as Fleming described it, a sumptuous menu. (Very much like today.) *En-route* the plane stopped at Orly and then Anchorage before arriving at Haneda some thirty or so hours after takeoff where he was met by Richard Lovelace Henderson (modeled as noted earlier on Richard Hughes). In the novel it took Bond an hour to get through customs, and the terminal is described as a madhouse. They drove into central Tokyo in a Toyopet saloon at what Bond thought was a suicidal speed while noting that on first appearances Tokyo did not look the most attractive city. Henderson replied that the Japanese do things back to front such as the light switches go up instead of down and that taps turn to the left.

(In fact this was possibly borrowed from James Kirkup's book *These Horned Islands* who writes, 'Many things go by opposites in Japan...door handles turn to the left instead of to the right, one presses light switches up instead of down, turns taps the opposite way to the way they are turned on in England.' An alternative source may have been the book *We Japanese. Being descriptions of many of the customs, manners, ceremonies, festivals, arts and crafts of the Japanese, besides numerous other subjects* published by the Fujita Hotel, which Fleming might well have bought on his first visit to Japan.)

Henderson went on to describe Tokyo as a 'bloody awful' place that suffers earthquakes every day, is battered by typhoons, and is either too hot or too cold. He moans too about the cost of

The Definitive Story Of You Only Live Twice

living, and suggests instead sticking to the back alleys. Tokyo is also described as having air full of fine dust because of demolition and reconstruction work. (In the run-up to the Olympics, much of central Tokyo was more akin to one vast construction site as sports facilities, expressways and hotels were built and old buildings demolished.)

At this point there is a mistake in the novel as it says they drove on the right whereas the rule in Japan has always been to drive on the left.

Arriving at the Hotel Okura they dive into the Bamboo Bar. This is not a real name although the hotel did feature a male-only bar known simply and accurately as the Men's Bar (but officially the Oak Room bar); alternatively they may have relaxed with a stiff drink at the Starlight Lounge on the hotel's roof, taking in a panoramic view of Tokyo.

The next night he and Henderson visit a bar in the Ginza called Melody. If there ever was, now there is no bar with that name in Ginza but, from Fleming's description, we know it was run by a black American (very possibly someone who had stayed in Tokyo after the US occupation or had come over later with the US Military and then decided to stay put) and was once a favourite hang-out for English ex-pats and journalists from the Foreign Correspondents Club. They drink Suntory whisky and Henderson says it is best to stick to the cheaper White Label (Suntory Shirofuda) blend. Bond is skeptical about the qualities of Japanese whisky; understandable at the time as the world class status of the drink had yet to be established.

If there is an inspiration for the man and bar it might be the black American actor Chico Lourant, an Army veteran who had stayed in Asia after the Korean War, and had taken up playing the trumpet in a Ginza club called The Crown Club during the early 1960s.

Fleming might also be making an oblique reference to Mecca -

mentioned in the Forward - a Tokyo bar where a grisly murder took place in the early 1950s.

From the bar they find an *izakaya* and eat eels (Fleming of course had enjoyed eel but no mention is made of whether Bond found them to his taste) and they then visit a whorehouse or perhaps one of Tokyo's plentiful bath and massage parlours. Fleming refers to it as 'The House of Total Delight' a name he made up but in the early to mid-1960s, as is still the case, there were hundreds if not thousands of delightful houses with many being found on the streets of Kabukicho.

After the *geisha* party, Tiger explains to Bond about Dr. Guntram Shatterhand.

Shatterhand's castle, he is told, is close by Fukuoka and faces the Tsushima Strait, 'the scene of the most famous defeat of the Russian Navy' when the Japanese Navy scored a decisive and important victory during the Russo-Japanese War of 1904-5. This had announced that Japan was now a world power to be reckoned with.

Bond is running out of his Moreland cigarettes and Tiger offers him the local brand Shinsei, which he finds to have a similar taste to American blends. Shinsei had been launched in 1949 and was a popular cheaper brand.

Tiger explains that Shatterhand had taken over and restored an isolated ruined castle, on a peninsula, one of many along this part of the Kyushu coastline built originally to ward off Korean invaders. This is not entirely true in that this northern coastline does not boast many castles and in fact no castles exist in Japan in isolated positions as they were positioned within settlements that then became castle towns, and centres of administration and commerce.

Fukuoka is described as a nest-bed of scoundrels - fascists, anarchists and members of secret societies like the Black Dragon Society, which had existed in real life. Shatterhand had recruited his own staff from former members of the society.

Tiger tells Bond that 25,000 Japanese commit suicide every year. Lovers link hands and throw themselves off the Kegon Falls at Nikko or run into the Mihara volcano on the island of Oshima. And now Shatterhand's poisonous garden was a favourite locale, with lovers from Tokyo taking the *Romancecar* express to Kobe, a boat trip across the Inland Sea to Beppo, a local train to Fukuoka and then a final walk to Shatterhand's Castle of Death.

Although there is no direct evidence, inspiration for this garden of death might have in part come from Seichō Matsumoto's 1960 novel *Kuroi Jukai* (Sea of Trees) set in the Aokigahara, the suicide forest at the base of Mount Fuji. The story follows two young lovers fated to die.

Japan still has one of the highest high suicide rates in the developed world, although on a *per-capita* basis it has declined since the 1960s even if the total numbers are similar.

In Japan, suicide is not a sin. Most suicides are not lovers but men - both old and young - and much of it is down to isolation and despair heightened by a culture where people tend to keep their feelings to themselves rather than sharing and seeking help.

Suicide too has been commonplace almost across Japan's long history. When Europeans first arrived in Japan in the 16 century they recorded that the Japanese had an indifferent attitude to death. And Tiger had trained as a *kamikaze* pilot. Still having a foreigner encourage suicide was not acceptable.

Tiger also talks about the Americanisation of Japan that had started after the country's defeat in the War. This was something that very much excised the Japanese as they saw the country being swamped by a way of life that was alien to their culture. Indeed, as Tiger points out Japan had not once in its history had to suffer the imposition of a new culture on their own by outside invaders.

Getting back to the task in hand, Tiger asks Bond to assassinate Shatterhand but in order to do this without discovery he must become Japanese and, more specifically, a deaf and dumb coal miner, the argument being that Bond's build has a resemblance to some coal miners.

And if Bondo-san is successful he will indeed give Britain access to Japanese intelligence.

Baby, the girl that Fleming encountered on his first trip, becomes Mariko Ichiban in the novel. She transforms Bondo-san into something resembling a Japanese miner (and whereas Fleming only enjoyed the Turkish sweat box and bath, Bondo-san of course enjoyed tricks on the side.)

Tiger and Bondo-san then undertake a slow journey to Fukuoka so that Tiger has the chance to train Bondo-san in the ways of the Japanese.

They start from Tokyo Station, which Fleming describes as thronged and packed with people mainly salarymen dressed in a button down white shirt, knitted black ties, and black trousers and shoes, taking the Expresso Gamagori - the gleaming orange and sliver express that Fleming had taken albeit on a different route. On the train, Bondo-san makes way for three woman and Tiger tells him angrily that this is decidedly not the Japanese way and that women have no priority in Japan.

Gamagori is painted as a pretty sea-side village with a humped island in the bay that housed an important shrine but they do not stop there but take the evening hydrofoil across the Ise Bay to the fishing port of Toba. Fleming describes this as an exhilarating 50 knot ride.

(The Hydrofoil service no longer operates but in the 1960s they had become popular on certain routes within Japan.)

To reach an inn, they walk through Toba's narrow streets hung with pretty paper banners and lanterns until they come to a small inn on the seafront from where they could see the statue of Mikimoto. After changing into *yukata*, they sip green tea and eat cake. Across Japan, inns and hotels will only accept guests after 3pm and after they change the very first thing that will happen is that a maid will bring tea and cake.

That night Bond and Tiger sit at a low table in their room and eat lobster, a speciality of the area along with rice, raw quails eggs in a sauce, sliced seaweed, rice and miso soup. Like Fleming, Bondo-san discovers that the lobster is still alive and moving.

Next day they visit the Outer Shrine of Ise. Bondo-san claps his hands three times and throws a coin onto the wire netting that would gather up the offerings.

Japan does not have a single national religion but shares two, Shinto and Buddhism. Shintoism has shrines and priests and was the indigenous religion of the country, while Buddhism has temples and monks and was introduced from China and Korea during the 6 century.

The Japanese are both religious and irreligious. Most observe and practice elements of both not least because almost everyone is buried using Buddhist rites but the practice of Shinto rites and visiting shrines is commonplace.

In both shrines and temples, there are *saisen* (wooden boxes) where worshippers throw coins as a symbolic offering to the gods before making their prayers - which are never spoken aloud.

Then Bondo-san and Tiger drive to Wadakin in Matsusaka on the road to Kyoto. It is described as an undistinguished hamlet and here Bondo-san gives a grateful cow a bottle of beer to drink, sprays and then rubs *shochu* into the cows flesh before driving to the owner's restaurant. Here Bondo-san is happy to sit on western chairs at a normal table and drink *sake* before trying the beef.

Wadakin has a distinguished history. Founded in 1878 by Kimbee Matsuda, he trained in restaurants such as Wadahei in Tokyo, before returning home to Matsusaka where he opened a beef restaurant in 1878. This proved to be a great success and in 1952, they established their own farm in Kawaimachi to supply *wagyu*.

Members of the royal family have eaten at the restaurant and Bondo-san (and Fleming) were not the only diners to visit from the field of literature. For example Takeshi Kaiko, a prominent novelist, wrote this in his book *Atarashii Tentai*,

...I haven't seen such high-quality hard charcoal lately. As that fine charcoal grew red hot and started glowing as though excited, a metal mesh was put over it, and the masterpiece was finally put on. It was indeed a true work of art...It cooked for a bit, just until it changed colour, at which point it was removed from the mesh, dipped in fresh soy sauce and eaten — my mouth filling with the aroma of milk and butter, the warm flavours and fragrance of this plump yet tender dish. So refined you could cut it with chopsticks, so tender, so hearty, so uncomplicated.

After lunch the two of them continue to a secret castle where Bondo-san was to be introduced to the arts of the ninja - or at least see Tiger's ninja in training.

Having arrived in Kyoto, Bondo-san and Tiger chose the Miyako Hotel. Here Bondo-san remains in his comfortable room and orders room service of Eggs Benedict and bourbon (Fleming's drink of choice), pleased that he is now sleeping, if only for one night, in a western-style bedroom. He turns on the TV and watches *The Seven Detectives* (*Shichinin no Keiji*), a popular TV series at the time.

Before driving to Kobe the next morning, they go briefly to the same ancient whorehouse that Fleming visited but Bondo-san was unimpressed.

From Kobe, they take the steamer directly to Beppu, sailing through the Seto Inland Sea. Their ship, the *Murasaki Maru*, is a recently constructed 3000-ton ship, which is part of the Kansai Kisen KK line, with all the luxuries of an ocean liner. (NB: Fleming may have made a mistake here as the *Murasaki's* usual route was from Kobe to Takamatsu.)

It takes a day to reach their destination - Fleming describing the Inland Sea as the equivalent of a 'long lake, with the ship throbbing grandly through endless horned islands.' (Nicely referencing James Kirkup's book.)

Tiger warns Bondo-san that whirlpools lurk between some of the islands - and he would have been referring to the Naruto whirlpools that lie between Honshu and Shikoku - although the *Muraski Maru* avoids sailing close to them.

The Seto Inland Sea is a body of water that separates the three main islands of Honshu, Shikoku and Kyushu; a sea that as it connects the Pacific Ocean to the Sea of Japan and thence to Korea and China has played for millennia a significant and strategic role in Japan's maritime and economic history.

During the 19 century, Bond and Fleming's former employer, the Royal Navy began to survey the Sea as the route through it was important for both warships and commercial traffic. The British Admiralty provides a detailed description of the Inland Sea in a contemporary account from the late 1860s:

'The great Inland Sea of Japan, called by the Japanese Seto Uchi is enclosed between the south-west coast of Nipon, which entirely bounds it on the north and east; and the islands of Kiusiu and Sikok, which bound it on the west and south.

It extends somewhat in an east and west direction, in length 240 miles, with a breadth varying from 3 to 30 miles. It has six divisions called *nadas* or seas, taking their names generally from the provinces, the coasts of which they wash; thus, the eastern part of the sea as far as Akashi Strait is called the Isumi Nada; and proceeding west, we have in succession the Harima Nada, Bingo Nada, Misima Nada, Iyo Nada and, lastly, Suwo Nada.

The Seto Uchi was first navigated fully by a British ship H.M.S. Cruizer in 1859. It contains upwards of 300 islands and rocks, with numerous shoals and dangers, and has a seaboard of nearly 700 miles, on which are situated numerous large towns and several of the provincial capitals; it abounds also with safe and convenient anchorages. It communicates with the Pacific by the Kii channel on the east, and by the Boungo channel, between Kiusiu and Sikok, on the south; and with the Sea of Japan by the strait of Shimonoseki on the west.

There is a great maritime trade along its populous shores as well as the through traffic to Osaka, one of the chief seats of commerce of the empire, and the seaport of its capital, Kioto.

The Seto Uchi can be navigated with safety at all seasons of the year and even under favourable circumstances during the night, the more particularly now that correct charts of it have been published.'

Consequently Commander Bondo-san was in a long line of Naval officers who had navigated this stretch of water.

To pass the time, when they are not eating and drinking, Tiger teaches Bondo-san about the nuances of *tanka* and *haiku* before they arrive in the town of Beppu at dusk.

Leaving their bags at a *ryokan* they visit the ten spectacular hells with their stinking sulfurous muds and geysers, belching great streams of red, blue and orange. Notices adorned with skull and cross bones warn visitors to keep a safe distance, which they do while waiting for one of the geysers to erupt, shooting grey boiling mud high into the air.

More commonly, it is said that there are eight of these hells (*jigoku*) and it is unlikely that they visited all of them in one evening as they are some distance from each other.

With some trepidation on Bond's part he is taken to eat *fugu*, at a restaurant close to the seafront - but before going out they slip into a *o-furo* bath, in a stark blue-tiled room then walk down the street and arrive at a restaurant where a giant blowfish sign hangs ominously above the door.

While waiting for the food to arrive, Tiger explains patiently to Bondo-san that the poison is contained in the liver and sex glands and, if eaten, kills instantly. Perhaps because of this knowledge, Bondo-san orders and swiftly knocks back five tumblers of *sake* - almost close to a bottle - and, not surprisingly after this amount of alcohol, he concludes that the fish tasted...well of nothing. In fact *fugu sashimi*, even without drinking vast quantities of *sake* is a delicate almost tasteless dish - but one always prettily arranged on a plate like white chrysanthemum petals, the flower of death.

Once the meal is finished, 'Bond sat back and lit a cigarette' and drank more hot *sake* now laced with blackened *fugu* fins. These are fins that have been grilled over a flame, known as *hirezaki*, and an essential element of any *fugu* meal, although its origin may be post World War 2.

The next day, they start out early so that they can begin the search for Shatterhand's castle near Fukuoka in the north west of the island. The drive would have taken about two hours from Beppu.

The castle and its garden lie on a small promontory that sticks out from the rocky coastline. Reaching the fortress by land without being detected was deemed impossible but it was believed that Bondo-san could enter via the seaward side by starting out from the small island of Kuro, home to *ama*.

As already noted, there is no *ama* island off Fukuoka and no island named Kuro. Instead Fleming had used as his inspiration Hekura Island, which had been described by Fosco Maraini in his book *The Diving Girls Island*. In turn this is more usually known in Japan as Hegurujima and can be found in the Sea of Japan off the Noto Peninsula.

To reach Kuro, Bond takes a police launch across the Sea of Genkai; and on reaching the island he is introduced to his host, the beautiful *ama* Kissy Suzuki, and her family. Once a Hollywood actress Kissy had decided that this was not the life for her and has returned to Japan disillusioned but she talks fondly of David Niven - perhaps a playful dig at the Bond film producers as Fleming had suggested that Niven play the role of Bond in the film *Dr No* rather than Sean Connery.

Kissy also explains that the islanders believe that the devil himself has come to live in the fortress but that a legend had already grown up on the island that their *Jizo* (the guardian god of children and *ama*) would send a *gaijin* (a foreigner) to slay the 'King of Death.'

Changing into his ninja suit, Bond swims to Shatterhand's fortress, hides and makes his plans to kill Blofeld and Irma Bunt.

The plan starts smoothly until Bond while creeping through the fortress, steps on floorboards designed as a trap, they spin round and he is cast in to a black hole. He has been caught, and despite his disguise and training in the ways of the Japanese, Bunt recognises him as James Bond. So much for Tiger's plan.

He is dragged away for tortuous questioning but eventually Bond is able to kill Blofeld, escapes from the castle moments before it blows sky-high because of an erupting geyser, and is rescued by Kissy and taken back to Kuro. (It is not made clear whether Bunt perished.)

Kissy realises that Bond has lost his memory due to the injuries he has sustained. She hides Bond in a cave in the belief that he will fail to regain his memory and that she and he will then remain blissful lovers for the rest of their lives.

Slowly his body mends; Dikko, Tiger and others had come to

The Definitive Story Of You Only Live Twice

the island in an attempt to discover the fate of Bond but the islanders neither reveal their secret nor his hiding place.

However, as a consequence of his injuries and amnesia, Bond has lost his sex drive. Kissy catches the mail-boat to Fukuoka, visits the local sex shop where she is able to obtain the sweat of a special toad that acts as an aphrodisiac. Some toad sweat does indeed contain the stimulant bofutenin which can act as an aphrodisiac and the Japanese also believe that *fugu* acts as one too. Obviously Kissy had found that oysters alone had not done the job.

To make doubly sure that she can revive Bondo-san's libido, Kissy buys a pillow-book of *shunga* pornographic engravings.

Shunga were banned in Japan for many years but had become popular during the Edo period when thousands of explicit paintings, prints, and illustrated books were produced, called 'spring pictures' (*shunga*). Many were known as 'pictures of the floating world' (*ukiyo-e*), and executed by some of Japan's most celebrated artists such as Utamaro and Hokusai, and were of a high quality.

The novel's final page has Kissy wondering how she will tell Bond that she is pregnant but as she ponders over this Bond announces that he must rediscover his past and that he thinks it might start in Vladivostok Russia. Kissy says she will take him to Fukuoka where he can catch a train to the northern island of Hokkaido and from there take a ferry to Sakhalin and finally a train to Vladivostok.

As mentioned earlier, the storyline and in particular this final chapter has echoes of *Madame Butterfly* the short story by John Luther Long where the American Naval Officer Pinkerton, marries a local girl on a temporary basis while in Japan, she falls pregnant and then he leaves. (This short story in turn was based on *Madame Chrysanthème* a novel by Pierre Loti, published in 1887.)

You Only Live Twice had received a mixed reception on its publication. Malcolm Muggeridge, a friend of Fleming, wrote a review in *Esquire*,

You Only Live Twice has a decidedly perfunctory air. Bond can only manage to sleep with his Japanese girl with the aid of colour pornography. His drinking sessions seem somehow desperate, and the horrors are too absurd to horrify ... it's all rather a muddle and scarcely in the tradition of Secret Service fiction. Perhaps the earlier novels are better. If so, I shall never know, having no intention of reading them.

His old friend Somerset Maugham had been sent a signed copy, and in turn had written a note saying that his own travelling days were sadly over, and he hoped that he could now see Fleming again.

This was not to be. On 11 August 1964 following dinner with a friend at his golf club, Fleming collapsed, and a few hours later died in the Kent and Canterbury Hospital. His life had been hanging by a thread for some time, yet he was at the height of success and only 56.

When he had left Haneda those two years earlier, he had turned to Hughes and Tiger and had said 'we are as only good as our friends.'

Hughes writing a piece about their travels together concludes by quoting the writer Basho,

Morning cold:

The voices of travelers

Leaving the inn.

SHATTERHAND

So what are the origins of the Shatterhand alias? Was there some clever meaning behind it? Or was Fleming up to his old tricks of taking the name from elsewhere? An old friend perhaps, or an acquaintance?

Blofeld first appeared in *Thunderball* when he is described as having a Polish father and a Greek mother. He studied at the University of Warsaw before attending the Warsaw Technical Institute to pursue further studies in engineering and radionics.

Before the start of the 2 World War, he sold secrets to the Third Reich but later moved to Turkey and sold secrets to the Allies as well.

In *Thunderball* he takes a backseat as the leader and founder of SPECTRE but he takes a bigger role in *On Her Majesty's Secret Service* and likewise in *You Only Live Twice*.

So why Shatterhand? And does his first name Guntram have any significance?

Dealing with this latter point first. Originally Fleming was going to call him Julius Shatterhand and in the manuscript this had been typed but then crossed out. This is understandable, as he had already called Dr No, Julius. Guntram too is a good strong European name and would fit the Blofeld character better.

And Shatterhand? Well indeed there is fictional character with the same name and that is Old Shatterhand who appeared as the main character in the novels written by the German Karl May, and set in the wild west of America. These were largely written in the 1890s and became immensely popular not just in German speaking countries but across the world.

May was a colourful character to say the least: he was jailed at least twice and was a dab hand at fraud. Just the sort of character that Fleming might warm to; when a child Fleming might well have read English translations of the Shatterhand novels. Perhaps also Fleming came across the works of May when he was studying in Austria, Munich and Geneva.

As the name is extremely rare, and yet was a well-known fictional character, a reasonable conclusion is that Fleming borrowed it from May.

THE CIA'S ASSESSMENT

In a conversation with Allen W Dulles in 1963, Fleming tells the now retired Director of the CIA, 'I've brought you into my next book [YOLT]. Comparing you favourably to your successor, who, I have said is a much more difficult man to get on with - from the *British*, of course, point of view.'

Dulles replies 'I hope not too difficult. Because I am supporting him every way I can.'

That successor was John McCone who had been appointed by President Kennedy - who had fired Dulles. McCone was an engineer, and did not have a background in intelligence but is said to have been a successful leader.

After *You Only Live Twice* had been published in the UK but before the August publication in the US, McCone was sent a memo from the Assistant to the Director for Public Affairs that highlighted the passages where the CIA and McCone had been mentioned.

It would seem that following the conversation with Dulles, Fleming had amended what he had written, and now said 'this

Graham Thomas

new man McCone...he's a good man alright and we get along well personally...' (This is M briefing Bond at the start of the novel, when he explains that the CIA under Dulles used to provide intelligence from the Far East but that has now stopped under McCone but only because the National Defense Council had told McCone to cease.)

As the publication went ahead unamended the CIA must have concluded that they would not try to pressure the publishers, New American Library, to make any changes.

Some years later, in a book edited by Dulles called *Great Spy Stories From Fiction,* he writes in an introduction that it is impossible to write about the Far East if the author hasn't been there and then mentions Fleming's visit to Tokyo in order to place Bond there.

THE FOOD

This chapter adds more detail about the food and drink that Bond consumed in *You Only Live Twice*, the nudge to include this topic coming from the excellent book by Edward Biddulph called *Licence to Cook: Recipes Inspired by Ian Fleming's James Bond*.

As he points out in his Introduction, food is very much part of the novels. He has also done the counting and says that on average there are five food references in the each novel. With at least nine references in *You Only Live Twice*, more if those not eaten by Bond are included, then this particular novel is a veritable feast.

In most of the novels Bond is a conservative eater: grilled sole, scrambled eggs, bacon, toast and marmalade for breakfast; lamb cutlets, fried chicken, roast duck, hamburgers and the such like for lunch or supper. Of course he enjoyed some expensive tastes: lobster and caviar being two examples. The fact that he appears to take to Japanese food with barely a murmur of complaint is therefore surprising as the closest he ever ate to Japanese food was smoked salmon - although Bond said he had a mania for it when it was of the highest quality. As O F Snelling pointed out in his book *007 James Bond A Report*, Bond had strong likes and disliked when it came to food, knowing what he liked and ensuring that he got it.

Japanese was decidedly exotic food. When the novel was written, the number of Japanese restaurants in London was zero.

It was only in 1967 that Hiroko was opened in St Christopher's Place off Oxford Street. It served traditional Japanese food including *sushi* and *sukiyaki* and, of course, hot *sake* was served. Why only one when now they are ubiquitous? Mainly because during the 1960s there were fewer than one thousand Japanese ex-pats living in London. Nor was there a Japanese grocery until Mikadoya opened in Dulwich also in 1967. (It should be noted for historical perspective that after the First World War when Japan was an ally, the Japanese population in London was big enough to sustain several restaurants but these closed during the Second World War.)

When the novel opens we learn that Bond is being described as an 8 flask *sake* man: that's likely to be the equivalent of two bottles of wine. This sobriquet was one to be relished as far from being an insult it was a compliment - so Tiger said.

As mentioned in the previous chapter *sake* was a cheaper rougher brew in the immediate decades after the War and not the sophisticated drink known today. Because of rice shortages, additives could be used to bulk out production: these included alcohol spirit, starch syrup, saccharine and amino acids. Hence the practice of drinking it warm thereby smoothing the rough edges introduced by these impurities.

Hughes said that drinking *sake* ensured they didn't argue across the duration of their trip. This is understandable as it is one of those drinks that is least likely to induce a hangover because of its inherent simplicity of rice, *koji* (a cooked fermented rice) and water (putting aside the additives!) Hence, while drinking 8 flasks is, for the normal drinker, certainly going to induce inebriation, it might be that at least the next day, tempers were not frayed.

The other thing about *sake* is that the Japanese believed then it was best drunk on an empty stomach, thereby ensuring that intoxication follows rather quickly. Slightly strange as some forty per cent of Japanese, along with other nations in the Far East, can easily get drunk as they lack the enzymes to properly digest alcohol. This is a genetic trait that leads to the liver failing to break down the byproducts of alcohol metabolism.

The next mention of food in the novel is Bond's plan to eat the new season's grouse and pink champagne at Scotts - a favourite eating hole for both Fleming and Bond where they shared the same table preference. Then, Scotts was to be found just off Piccadilly on Coventry Street. It was known as an elegant restaurant decorated with engraved glass and with the air of Victorian dignity, although I wonder if, in later years, either men were pleased that on the restaurant's facade was an illuminated sign for the common or garden Woodbine cigarette.

Now I am not a fussy person when it comes to wine pairings. Rigid rules are not to be broken but to be ignored completely unless of course it is adding cola to claret. Champagne can be drunk across a whole meal although the sweetness, richness and body need to reflect the nature of the dish. To drink rose champagne with grouse requires it to be a full bodied vintage. In short it has to possess heft. Perhaps one of the early 1950s or late 40s was chosen from one of Bond's favourite house such as Cliquot, Dom Perignon, Krug, Pommery, and Taittinger.

It was after that dinner that Bond caught a JAL flight to Tokyo commentating later that *en-route* he had eaten six dinners. This is possibly not an exaggeration as the route was the London – Copenhagen – Anchorage – Tokyo polar route. He would have certainly eaten six meals: breakfasts, lunch, dinners and snacks over a period of at least 24 hours flying.

Looking at a JAL menu from the period there was ample opportunity to stick to Western food as the choice was extensive. This is not surprising. Most of the passengers would have been westerners as the Japanese government still placed restrictions on overseas travel, which was limited to business, government officials, technical study missions or sporting teams. There was little need, therefore, to feature Japanese food on the menu.

I have been able to locate a 1970 menu for a JAL trans-Pacific flight and interestingly by then they were serving both hot and cold *sake* reflecting the revolution in *sake* brewing and a return to the old style without additives thereby creating much more refined sakes. The menu itself included dishes such as seafood cocktail, *pate de fois gras*, *tournedos*, braised chicken, Mandarin Pudding, and cheese cake.

The first mention of a Japanese meal in the novel is when Bond eats raw octopus (*tako*) on rice. Whether Fleming really means raw octopus is a moot point. Octopus is more usually boiled to both make it tender and to bring out the flavour. The flesh is then thinly sliced as shown in the photograph on the preceding page. In this form it might well be mistaken for being raw as it has a delicate taste and is almost translucent. More commonly eaten raw is cuttlefish (*ika*) that is often cut into thin strips and has a bite to it. And rather like the lobster that I will come onto next, cuttlefish can also be served live.

I also wonder whether Fleming was describing *tako* sushi, which is a popular sushi dish rather than octopus eaten with a bowl of rice.

The infamous live lobster that both Fleming and Bond ate is only a slight exaggeration. While in the photo below the live lobster seems to be still, it is the most common way to eat lobster *sashimi* in order to present it in perfect condition. In truth while the lobster has not been boiled to kill it, the main nerve has been cut through and the lobster is in fact dead. The movement is down to the twitching of nerves - or at least that is what I have been told. Bond ate this with sliced seaweed or *nori,* and raw eggs broken over rice, a common dish in Japan. The sauce that Fleming mentions might well have been a dash of *mirin* flavoured light soy or perhaps a *dashi* based sauce.

Sticking to seafood, Kissy of course was diving for abalone or *awabi*. This can be cooked over a fire when the flesh is in the shell, or it can be removed and sliced for *sashimi*.

One of the most endearing treats of Japanese hospitality is to be served green tea and sweetmeats when first arriving at a *ryokan* - and sometimes at the very best hotels. Green tea of course is unsweetened and has a naturally bitter taste that is offset by the dainty Japanese sweets or small cakes. More often than not, these will be local delicacies.

In complete contrast to the sweets, *wagyu* beef is rich simply because it has a lot of marbled fat. Fleming says that it was eaten with blood sauce, which I find baffling as I have never come across this. Other side dishes might would have been vegetables, grated *daikon* (to cut through the fat), salad, pickles. My own favourite is Olive Beef that can only be found in Kagawa Prefecture, and is named this because the cattle are fed on an olive mash.

Then comes the dreaded *fugu* with Bond knocking back at least five flasks of sake before eating the supposedly deadly flesh. Besides the sliced flesh, he was served it deep fried and most likely was given the roe and some of the flesh served in a hot broth. Plus at the end of the meal he drank more sake with blackened *fugu* fin.

Rice with flecks of fish is a typically frugal rural dish. Across time, the Japanese have been frugal eaters, and many of the older generation still are. Rice of course is the mainstay of their diet. Even the generic for meal - *gohan* - is the same word as steamed rice, and eating a bowl of rice with some topping is a still a popular dish eaten for breakfast, lunch or dinner

Another frugal dish is plain rice with a raw egg broken over it, often eaten with tofu sprinkled with soy served in a separate dish.

At the end of the novel Bond appears to have ceased drinking. I am not surprised after the amount he had consumed. However, if he had not hit the wagon, it is usual to drink beer and not sake with the last meal that was mentioned *sukiyaki*. Although there was no recipe given the dish would have included more vegetable than meat and these would have included cabbage, tofu, and often noodles. All the ingredients are added to a soy broth, which is quite sweet. Once cooked the beef is often dipped into a bowl of whipped raw egg before being eaten.

Japanese beer is and was dominated by brands from the big breweries with Kirin dominating all of them. In the 1960s they were producing pasteurised products, and mostly a bitter pale lager with hoppy notes.

It is likely that he could also find Japanese whiskey on the island, and so if the beer wasn't too his taste perhaps whiskey was more palatable.

PRODUCTION STARTS

Two years after the publication of the book, filming of *You Only Live Twice* started in July 1966.

The previous Bond films had remained reasonably faithful to the books' plots but *You Only Live Twice* was the first to move away from the novel. In part this was because the book, the third of a Blofeld trilogy, carried on from where *On Her Majesty's Secret Service* left off and, for a number of reasons, OHMSS had not yet been filmed. Most crucially at the end of OHMSS, Bond marries Tracy and she is then killed by Blofeld and Irma Bunt, which sends Bond into his depression that we see at the start of YOLT and which ultimately leads to his revenge killing of both Blofeld and Bunt.

Clearly this would make no sense as a plot line if OHMSS had not been filmed. As well, the producers thought that the novel was rather prosaic (castles and dangerous gardens) and, of course, much of the novel concerned itself with a journey across Japan when little action took place. (Although it could have been turned into a classic chase, with Bond pursued by Blofeld's men.)

On the other hand the simple essence of the novel is retained: SPECTRE is at the heart of the story, Bond is ordered to Japan, and works with the Japanese secret service to assassinate Blofeld while being disguised as a Japanese, key characters are featured, and Bond undergoes an arranged marriage with an *ama* girl to help provide further cover. Bond is taught in the way of the Ninja, and they even traverse from Tokyo down to Kyushu albeit in seconds.

The first draft of a screenplay was written by Sydney Boehm an American screenwriter known for his drama films. This was more an early treatment to get the film's production off the ground, and he was then replaced by Harold Jack Bloom who in turn was replaced by the author Roald Dahl - though some of Bloom's ideas were retained.

Dahl claimed that when he was offered the job after meeting the two producers Cubby Broccoli and Harry Saltzman they had not mentioned that Bloom's screenplay already existed. He only found out when they asked that certain elements of this previous script be retained such a Bond's fake death and burial at sea, and the idea that Blofeld was pitting the Americans against the Russians by kidnapping their space craft. After some argument between the producers and Bloom's agent, Bloom was given the credit of 'Additional Story Material.' (And later Bloom was to claim that much of what was on the screen stemmed from his original ideas, although Dahl was adamant this was not the case.)

Some maintain that this was Dahl's first experience of writing a screenplay but this is untrue as he had previously written two episodes for the *Alfred Hitchcock Presents* TV show, and just before his involvement on *You Only Live Twice* he had also written the screen play for a film *The Bells of Hell Go Ting-a-Ling-a-Ling*. This was another United Artists production (all James Bond films to date had been distributed by UA), was to star Gregory Peck with cameras planned to roll before *You Only Live Twice*. However although *The Bells of Hell Go Ting-a-Ling-a-Ling* started shooting in the summer of 1966 it was abandoned in August after Dahl had left for Japan to work on *You Only Live Twice*. Dahl later said that the Head of UA, David Picker, had been impressed

The Definitive Story Of You Only Live Twice

by how he had written a story from nothing for *The Bells of Hell Go Ting-a-Ling-a-Ling*, and had suggested to Broccoli and Saltzman that they consider using him.

Initially Dahl was a reluctant Bond writer and was open that he was doing it for the money not least because his wife, the actress Patricia Neal, had suffered a series of strokes and was unable to work. According to one Dahl biography, he told his publisher that he found the idea 'exceptionally distasteful.'

Dahl thought the novel plain boring with no dramatic structure and one of Fleming's worse books. (It is worth noting though that up until Fleming died the two had remained close friends since the Second World War.) Hence it was agreed that the plot had to reflect the exciting world of the mid 1960s. The producers and Dahl realised the attraction to cinema audiences of utilising the burgeoning space race between Russia and the US and so kept Bloom's idea and, with excitement about the Tokyo Olympics still in the air they realised that the novel's Japan setting would be precisely the sort of exotic location that audiences craved.

As noted earlier, the film version creates a new story (although one that isn't quite so removed as some claim), which in truth is a rehash of *Dr No* and *Thunderball* dotted with previous Bond set-pieces: evil man hijacks rockets (instead of a plane); holds the world to ransom, is tracked down by Bond and killed. Throw in a car chase, some hi-tech gadgets (such as Little Nellie, and rocket firing cigarettes) and a big set piece in the final reel where the villain's lair is blown sky high and this was obviously not a huge creative challenge for Dahl.

Indeed, he once commented that all he needed to do for the final set piece was write 'fight in a volcano.' This he also readily admitted in an article *The Oriental Beauties of You Only Live Twice*, published in the June 1967 issue of *Playboy* magazine, when he explained that yes, he wrote the script to a formula already established in the previous films, and yes he never took the script seriously.

This formula was mandatory, he was told by the producers when they first met. It had to be total cinematic experience that was suitable for the family: action, exotic locations, stunts and great music included. One of the most important elements, Dahl was told, was to always have three Bond girls: the first was on Bond's side - before she was killed. The second was the enemy - before she was killed; and the third would be Bond's friend, would not be killed under any circumstances, and at the end of the film would end up in a suggestive embrace.

Another missing ingredient from the novel was the vulnerable and emotional side to Bond's personality and the dark truths that Fleming had started to expose in the book. Most likely, with the success of *Thunderball*, the producers may well have felt they wanted to keep the machismo thuggish element to Bond.

So while it might be excusable because of the sequencing of the films, it is a pity that *You Only Live Twice* has not been made in a version closer to the novel because indeed it has the potential to show a different side to Bond, that he is not invincible, that he can suffer doubt like everyone else.

Despite the restrictions and simplicity of the plot, Dahl did admit later that working on *You Only Live Twice* was the only film experience he'd enjoyed. 'The script of my Bond film is my only good experience. Usually, you don't end up with a line of your dialogue left.' His first draft had taken eight weeks to write but inevitably went through revisions. These were taken from Gypsy House Great Missenden where Dahl lived, to London in a chauffeur-driven Rolls-Royce.

By 17 June 1966, a final screenplay had been delivered to the producers.

How much of the pure spectacle originated with Dahl is open to question: Ken Adam says he came up with the idea of Blofeld's lair being inside a volcano as Bloom's original idea was to have Bond disguised as a Japanese miner (as in the novel) with Blofeld's lair being a salt mine. However both Broccoli and Lewis Gilbert's recollections suggest that they all made an initial contribution and Broccoli always said that ideas for all the films came from many people; Broccoli's wife Dana had the idea of a moving car being picked up by a giant magnet suspended from a helicopter, and Little Nellie was a late inclusion after it's inventor was heard being interviewed in a radio programme.

None the less, the wonderfully manic imagination of Dahl is scattered everywhere so that almost every scene has a unexpected dramatic device inserted: from poison being dripped down a length of thread, to the bridge that dumps errant villains into a piranha pool. Dahl had also discarded other distractions: for example, this is the first movie where Bond does not check into a hotel - even though at one point he does reveal that he is staying in the Tokyo Hilton. Nor does Universal Export make an appearance.

The director was Lewis Gilbert, highly experienced but shooting his first Bond film. The renowned Freddie Young was on camera, and the all-important second unit photography was led by Peter Hunt and the cameraman Bob Huke.

The initial plan proposed three weeks of principal shooting at Pinewood, a total of eight weeks in Japan and then a further ten weeks back in Pinewood, with everything to be wrapped by the end of November. In the end the production ran over into 1967.

The production team (including Broccoli, Gilbert, Adams, Hunt plus screenwriter Bloom) started scouting for locations in February 1966. Torao 'Tiger' Saito had given them the itinerary from when he, Hughes and Fleming had travelled through Japan to research the novel.

The team spent about three to four weeks in Japan and split in two: one team went looking for salt mines, while the second team flew the length and breadth of Japan looking for a castle with gardens, by the sea - which they never found of course because no such thing exists in the form they were looking for. They were on a wild goose chase and one wonders if this was deliberate. After all, 'Tiger' Saito or any Japanese historian or expert would have been able to tell them immediately that Fleming's castle was fanciful. In fact there are only twelve ancient castles standing in Japan, none like the castle described by Fleming, and it would have been clear that the only solution was to build a set.

'One of the most memorable Bond films,' said Ken Adams in an interview, 'from my point of view, was *You Only Live Twice*... so we rented two helicopters when we got to Tokyo and covered, I think, two-thirds of Japan during three or four weeks.

'I was flying with Lewis Gilbert, the director, and in the other one there was Freddie Young, the cameraman, with Cubby Broccoli, and we didn't find any of the Fleming locations because... I'm not sure whether he was there or whether he had invented these locations, but they didn't exist, like certain castles and gardens, poisonous gardens and so on. So we were getting really quite desperate about them, and during our last week we were on the island of Kyushu...and by chance we flew over an area of volcanoes who... I mean...the image was fantastic, like a moonscape or something...I think it was Lewis who said 'Wouldn't it be fun if our villain has his headquarters in one of these extinct volcanoes', and the idea appealed to me enormously, and I immediately did a little scribble which I showed to Lewis and Cubby, and they liked it.'

However, Lewis Gilbert later said that in fact they had been in discussion with Richard Hughes. He had told them of their visit to Mt Aso, how Fleming having had the idea to use the volcano as a setting, eventually decided that having Shatterhand set up camp there was too fantastical and had dropped the idea. This, said Gilbert, was the genesis for the idea.

The Definitive Story Of You Only Live Twice

Building of the volcano set started in May even before a single frame of film had rolled through the camera, although it would not be used until after the crew returned from location filming.

Back in the UK Adams started work designing the other sets. They had returned with reference photographs for the Japanese interiors that were to be built at Pinewood only to discover that some of the materials were hard to source in England...such as big flat stones for the bathhouse, although eventually a beach in Cornwall provided them.

After Dahl had finished his first draft of the script - including the volcano as the villain's lair - more locations were scouted in Japan during May, and Toho one of Japan's major studio's was appointed as the local partner – not least as they were the Bond film distributors in Japan. They lent their young producer Kikumaru Okuda to act as the technical advisor for all things Japanese. Okuda-san had been co-producer the year before on the Japanese-US film *None but the brave* directed by Frank Sinatra and so was well-versed in the Western ways of making films.

While in Japan, Broccoli and Gilbert held a press conference in Tokyo to announce with great fanfare that the next James Bond movie was going to be filmed in Japan.

The critical role of Tiger was handed to Japanese actor Tetsuru Tamba who Gilbert had worked with before and who he thought was an obvious choice as besides his acting abilities he was well-respected in the Japanese film industry and would act as a father figure to the other Japanese cast members. Gilbert also noted that he was a karate expert. His English lines were subsequently dubbed by Robert Rietti, although his own voice is used when he speaks in Japanese, and is clearly a different voice.

As part of this second recce' they started casting for the two Japanese Bond girls in a studio also provided by Toho Films. Founded in 1932, Toho was (and is) one of the major Japanese film companies, most famous in the Western world for the *Godzilla* films, and was well-placed to be of help locally. Choosing the two Japanese Bond girls was not straightforward because of the all pervasive lack of English language ability but eventually they cast the locally popular Akiko Wakabayashi who had not only appeared in Japanese films but three European films including the German production *The Girl From Hong Kong* in which she starred, and Mie Hama who proved to be less confident in English and ended up being dubbed by Nikki Van der Zyl, a stalwart of dubbed Bond girls. Both girls were contracted to Toho Studios and had already appeared in films since the late 1950s. One film they had both starred in was a faux James Bond thriller called *Kokusai himitsu keisatsu: Kagi no kagi (Key of Keys)*. It is sometimes claimed incorrectly that they starred in a Woody Allen film together but in fact *Kokusai himitsu keisatsu: Kagi no kagi* was a Toho production taken up by an American producer who decided that it could be turned into a comedy spoof by over-dubbing completely new English dialogue. The producer chose Allen to do this - no new footage was shot and the Japanese actors had no inkling that they would appear in this over-dubbed film.

Hama had been born in Tokyo on 20 November 1943 but her father's small factory was burnt down during in World War II and she grew up poor. She left school as soon as she could and was working as a ticket puncher on a Tokyu Corporation bus aged 16, when Toho discovered her. He film debut was in 1960 in *Young Skin*.

Wakabayashi too had been born in Tokyo, on 13 December 1939 but she joined Toho after applying for a couple of roles when still a student at Tokyo Metropolitan Aoyama High School. Over 3000 girls had applied for a role in Kurosawa's *Hidden Fortress* released in 1958 but only five girls were selected. She is not credited in the film but most likely appeared as a slave girl. She also appeared uncredited in *Tokyo Holiday* but her first credited role was in *Song for the Bride*, directed by Ishiro Honda (the creator of *Godzilla*), which also appeared in 1958.

They had already cast the European girl who would play Blofeld's assistant. Towards the end of June, over fifty girls had been selected for an initial interview, some of this taking place at The Dorchester Hotel for publicity purposes, and a dozen or so were then screen tested but the final choice of the flamed-haired German actress Karin Dor was easy to make according to Lewis Gilbert. (Although in fact she was not flamed hair at all - her hair had to be dyed for her appearance as she was a natural brunette and the producers wanted her hair colour to be distinct from the two Japanese actresses.)

Shooting of interior shots began on Stage E, Pinewood Studios on Monday 4 July 1966. The opening Hong Kong set bedroom scene took up the first two days of shooting; on Wednesday and Thursday they switched to Henderson's scenes at his immaculately recreated Japanese home. While the interior is without fault, there is a fluff in the dialogue. The film is clearly set in the present that is 1966-7 but first Henderson says he lost his leg in Singapore in 1942 but a couple of lines later claims he has been living in Japan for 28 years - in other words since 1939. (Also he would have been ejected from the country as soon as the War with Japan started.) Henderson also famously offers Bond a martini that has been stirred not shaken, which Bond readily accepts - but this should be put down to Dahl's mischievous mind. On the other hand, it is generally accepted now that for a better drink, martinis should definitely be stirred and not shaken.

On Friday 8 July they were working on the scenes in the Osato offices (in Tokyo), which had been built on Stage D. For those with good eyes there is a samurai costume on display, which might be a nod to Shatterhand's outfit in the novel.

Shooting these scenes continued into the second week before they filmed the interior scenes of Tiger's office, and the scenes with M and Miss Moneypenny on a submarine - when she tosses

Graham Thomas

Bond a copy of *Instant Japanese: A Pocketful of Useful Phrases* by Masahiro Watanabe and Kei Nagashima.

Dahl was on-set and even as they shot, he was doing rewrites, usually deleting lines to make the delivery shorter and crisper.

CONNERY ON LOCATION

On 25 July the production crew left for Tokyo. Separately the second unit had been filming in Hong Kong: the street scene in Kowloon, using Shantung Street off the Nathan Road (look out for the crowd of onlookers stood on the pavement); the wide shots of Victoria Harbour and the Star Ferry; and the shady foreign agent sitting in the Hong Kong Yacht Club, watching the burial of Bond in the harbour while reading the news of his death in the *Hong Kong Standard* and drinking a glass of white wine. (The actual committal was not filmed in Hong Kong but at sea off Gibraltar, which is why the skyscrapers disappear from the background. At an even greater distance from Hong Kong was the retrieval of the corpse - this was filmed in the Bahamas. For such a short sequence it might win a record for having the most geographically spread locations.)

Nor was Connery filmed in Hong Kong. Instead he and his wife Diane Cilento had left their home in Acton, flew to Bangkok for three days, staying in the Erawan Hotel, then one of the city's top hotels. Here Connery (or was it Bond?) had to endure a press conference where he was asked whether the Bond films were contributing towards the violence that could be found in Thai society. (He replied a polite no.)

Finally the pair arrived at Haneda in the early morning 27 July having taken a Pan-Am flight. Here they faced mayhem with fans, journalists and police jostling in the arrivals hall: Bond and Connery hysteria had gripped Tokyo. This was all captured by the British journalist and TV broadcaster Alan Whicker who had accompanied the crew to film a documentary about the making of the film, as an episode of his BBC television series *Whicker's World*.

(Whicker had met with the producer of the films, Cubby Broccoli and Harry Saltzman in London and found them enthusiastic about the project idea - after all any publicity was good publicity - and he was given *carte blanche* to follow the production.)

Connery and Cilento were bundled into the back of a black limo' and whisked off to central Tokyo while an all-girl white-gloved brass band played a military march on the tarmac. By now a new highway had been built into the centre of Tokyo and so they were taken at speed to the Tokyo Hilton pursued by the media in five cars. ('Now listen it up' as Q might say. Without making reading complicated it should be noted that this 'old' Hilton is now the Capitol Tokyu Hotel, and a new Hilton was built elsewhere in 1984. Like other international hotels, the Hilton had been built in preparation for the Tokyo Olympics and had opened in 1963 as the first internationally branded hotel in Tokyo. In 2008, the 'old' Tokyu hotel was itself replaced with a brand new building.)

As soon as they arrived, Connery was again engulfed by the press who crowded-out the lobby. Despite requests, they refused to leave and Connery felt he could not even go for lunch but stayed in his suite (rather strangely Broccoli had taken the appropriately numbered 1007). Relenting eventually, he and Diane visited the adjacent Hie shrine. They were followed through the *Torii* and up the steps by journalists and photographers who Whicker describes as a mob of small darting men, all wearing identical dark blue suits and white nylon shirts, and almost dragged to the ground by the weight of their enormous telephoto lenses.

Whicker had already come to the conclusion - as did some if not most of the cast - that Connery had become irritated by his worldwide fame, bored and indifferent to the films. As if to demonstrate this, at the afternoon press conference he arrived *sans* socks, tie and toupee, determined to be seen as Sean Connery and not James Bond. Questions ranged from whether he thought the newly released *Casino Royale* film with Peter Sellers and David Niven would spoil the Bond franchise (no he said) and did he know anything about the new 'moth' fashion. His reply was he'd never heard of it and did the questioner mean Mod. Moth, he is told.

That night Bond, his wife and a small group including Whicker shot out of the Hilton in their limo' to go eat in a Japanese restaurant off the Ginza, an uncomfortable drive because of pursuing cameramen in cars and on motorbikes. Outside the restaurant they had to manhandle themselves through a forest of lenses. Even in the restaurant, despite best efforts by the owner, photographers sneaked in and took photographs as Connery drank Kirin beer, ate crab salad and Kobe steak. Whicker sympathised with Connery who replied that being hounded wasn't only happening in Tokyo but at their house in Acton, London. 'We have a marvellous house in Acton,' Connery says, 'in a wonderful situation in a cul-de-sac [in fact Centre Avenue] by Acton park but there are some real head cases around.'

With dinner finished, they left to discover that the streets around the restaurant were rammed with jostling fans held back by grimacing police.

Kagoshima

The next day Connery and the crew - augmented by a Japanese crew - flew first to Osaka Airport and then by helicopter south to Kagoshima Prefecture where the bulk of the Japanese exteriors were to be filmed. They were joined by Roald Dahl, on hand again to make any last minute script adjustments, as well as Whicker and his own film crew.

On arrival, Alan Whicker checked into the luxury Shigetomi-so, one of Kagoshima's most stunning ryokan and already chosen as the location for Tiger Tanaka's home. Ken Adam is quoted by Whicker as saying, 'We're staying at this bloody awful hotel in town and Whicker's living in luxury in our set...' The ryokan had been a villa of the Shimazu *daimyo* for several hundred years and was often used by distinguished guests visiting the region. When Whicker arrived he was greeted at the entrance by the hostess and then shoes removed shown to his room where he changed into a crisp white *yukata*...and relaxed.

(The ryokan is now known as the Shimazu Shigetomisoh Manor House and is primarily used as a wedding venue.)

That bloody awful hotel where Ken Adam, Sean Connery and the rest of the crew stayed was the Shiroyama Kanko Hotel in Kagoshima City and it was from here that they would take cars to Shigetomi-so, or a helicopter to the tiny fishing village of Akime, and the volcanoes of the national Park.

Dahl was to later comment about his time on location and how at the close of the day, the cast and crew would relax with a cold beer on set. Connery was part of the crowd but as Dahl observed,

'He was the only man making a million in the film and he never stood anyone a round. This was known. They all talked about it. He is not an attractive personality.'

He also had something to say about Connery's acting,

'We went out of our way to give him quips that were incredibly clever, but they only had to be spoken with a straight poker face. There was damn little acting for him to do. He walked through it, you know. Literally.'

In fact from reading all his comments over the years, he clearly did not warm to Connery at all, and this may well have coloured his view of the star.

Akime

The village of Akime - across the other side of the peninsula and about 30 kms from where they were staying - was the principle location for Bondo-san's new-found life as a married man living with Kissy. Here Kissy spent her days diving, and several of the scenes included the presence of beautiful pearl divers who in fact were a nine young actresses from Tokyo including Kikko Matsuoka, and a lift attendant from the Tokyo Hilton. Naturally it was thought the girls would be happy to be filmed in bikinis but three of the girls initially refused and it took some persuading to make them relent. Persuasion being money.

As Broccoli was quickly to find out, a combination of the heat that exceeded 100F, humidity, the ever present media that harassed Connery and the crew, the difficulty of negotiating local bureaucracy, and the Japanese way of doing business meant that shooting here was far from easy.

To make matters worse the press also put around stories that the production company would fail to pay their bills before leaving, which irked Broccoli no end. 'This is terribly unfair,' he said.

As the American service newspaper *Stars & Stripes* wrote at the time,

'The tiny fishing village of Akime, on the southernmost tip of Japan, will never be the same again.

James Bond and company have descended upon it by helicopters, buses and air-conditioned cars. They have a mobile snack bar (sandwiches, lime juice, tea and water) and a built-in-a-bus restroom on the set at all times.

And when superstar Sean Connery, *sans* trench coat, tricky

Graham Thomas

attaché case and made-up to look like a Japanese fisherman, strides unsmilingly toward the camera, he is besieged by a battalion of Japanese photographers...

The Japanese press — *en masse* — has submitted formal complaints to publicity people and co-producer Albert "Cubby" Broccoli because they don't feel they are getting enough photographs or personal interviews with the star.

Although the straw hat sales and the amount of beer peddled across the counter in Akime's only hotel have skyrocketed, the villagers are only mildly impressed.

Fishing nets them several million yen a year and on weekends they always attract at least 300 fishermen and swimmers a day.'

Shigetomi-so nestles on the side of a hill and is the most luxurious of ryokan, with lush gardens and sweeping views out to sea and across to the active volcano on Sakarujima. The scene with Bond, Mie and Tiger in the garden was the first location sequence to be shot after they arrived. They sit at a table and Bond and Tiger drink Suntory Old Whisky, a malt blend launched in 1950 as a premium product in the Suntory range.

Scenes were then shot around Akime: in the harbour, in the bay and at the some nearby outcrops on the small uninhabited island Okiakime where a cave was found (and given the name Rosaki Cave in the film), and where nasty gas escapes. It is here too that the earlier scene of Bond emerging from the sea and entering Japan for the first time was filmed. Kissy's house on a hillside can still be seen although it has been modernized, as well as the alley and stairs that she and Bond walk up to reach it. (The owners of the house have erected a small board with photos from the film and they are happy to point out locations.)

It has been claimed that the media and local villagers in Akime were happy to see the departure of the film crew. As was referred to earlier the shooting in Kyushu had caused some problems with the residents. One example cited was that the production team had tried to change the appearance of Akime to make it look like a quaint Meiji Era village rather than how it looked now.

We might think that desirable but of course the locals wanted their village to look modern and their new homes and buildings not covered by wood. There was the incident when Gilbert asked what the press reported as a local high school girl extra to expose her body more than she had agreed to. (Although in many other references the dozen or so extras used as pearl divers were said to have come from Tokyo and certainly one was the young actress Matsuoka Kiko, born February 11, 1947 who went on to do quite a lot of TV work, and then became a game show talento.) However some more recent testimony from locals around at the time recount that they were pleased to have the crew there.

Mount Shinmoe

Eventually, Bond discovered Blofeld's lair under the crater on Mount Shinmoe, a mountain 4659 feet high and topped with a water-filled crater, 2459 feet in diameter. Filming took place here around 10 August with Connery, Mie Hama and Tetsuro Tamba and extras on top of the mountain.

In the film we see them climbing through dense forest to reach the mountain top but in fact they were brought to the summit by helicopter. Nonetheless in the sweltering heat and humidity, Mie Hana passed out one day and she had to be rushed off the mountain by the helicopter. But the very next day she was back in front of the cameras.

The final sequence shot in southern Kyushu was Q's explanation of the workings of Little Nellie to Bond before he takes his first flight in the gyrocopter. The assembly of Little Nellie was shot in Pinewood but its take-off was filmed in Tenpozancho, Kagoshima, around 8 August.

The first unit and actors then left for Kobe while the second unit directed by Peter Hunt, used Mount Shinmoe's lonely crater as the exterior of Blofeld's headquarters; here they filmed 100 ninja tumbling over its edge on ropes - before cutting to the Ken Adam's volcano built on the back-lot of Pinewood in far away Buckinghamshire.

Kobe

The cast and crew stopped briefly in Kobe No 3 dock in Kobe - in the *novel* a fight takes place on Dock 8 - with a hastily renamed ship standing in for the *Ning-Po* the ship that was bringing rocket fuel ingredients to Osato. This was filmed in 16 August with special precautions taken to protect the crew from the local *yakuza* but this did not stop a thrilling tracking shot from a helicopter over warehousing and ships.

Himeji

Then they moved on to Japan's celebrated Himeji castle in the third week of August where they intended to film all of the ninja training scenes. However after some initial set-ups they were asked to stop because it was found that damage was being done to one of the ancient walls from the ninja weapons that were being thrown at the cut-out villains. This led to some scenes being filmed later in Tokyo and the Japan-side producer Hiroshi Nezu having to make deep apologies to the Himeji Castle Management Office. It is worth noting here, that some of the ninja sequences featured martial arts that were pure fiction. This led to some controversy and many of the few authentic practitioners deciding not to get involved. However two sword masters, Katzutora Toyoshima and Tomoo Koide are featured.

Nachi

Their final location outside of Tokyo was Mount Nachi - in the Yoshino-Kumano National Park - where Bond's wedding to Kissy takes place at the beautiful, serene and ancient Kumano Nachi Taisha shrine complex. This was on 25 and 26 August, and one hundred and twenty extras were brought to the shrine. It is true to say that these scenes unlike the ninja depictions, accurately capture the essence of a *Shinto* wedding.

After the filming had finished on the first day, the cast and crew celebrated Connery's thirty-sixth birthday by bringing a birthday cake on set, before they went on to the Nakanoshima Hotel for a birthday dinner, drinks and some dancing, which possibly explains why in some shots he appears a little weary. Connery turned up wearing a yukata, and the music was provided by a student band, who happened to be staying at the hotel.

Scenes where we see Bond and Kissy climbing through dense forests and tumbling waterfalls to reach Blofeld's volcano lair were filmed in the park itself before the first unit returned to Tokyo, with Connery taking the opportunity to take the *Shinkansen*.

Tokyo

Back in Tokyo the first scenes shot in the city with Connery were outside the Hotel New Otani whose exterior was used as the headquarters of the Osato Corporation (and its revolving Cocktail Lounge had been the inspiration for Osato's office back in Pinewood).

The New Otani had opened in September 1964 - just before the start of the Tokyo Olympics. The original hotel is the building featured in the film - as since then further extensions and towers have been added - and the second unit crew stayed at the hotel during the filming of *You Only Live Twice* sequences shot in Tokyo.

Here we see a long shot of a Brantly helicopter landing on the helipad, Osato and his assistant leaving the helicopter (Dor had flown to Tokyo just for this one brief shot), Bond's escape from the offices with Aki, and later his return to meet with Mr Osato himself, and once again another escape, both times in a uniquely adapted Toyota 2000GT sports car. Often referred to as a convertible this is off the mark as the car was a modified version of the hardtop coupe as no convertible was manufactured; the modification was to cut off the roof and add a fake *tonneau* cover for the simple fact that because of the car's dimensions it was impossible for Connery (and his stunt double) to fit in the vehicle.

By the time the film was shot, Japanese car manufacturers had begun to make their presence felt on the world market and the 2000 had been produced primarily to show the world that Toyota could make more than just dinky family saloon cars. (And, for that matter dinky little sports cars as they were already producing the 2 cylinder Toyota Sport 800.) The 2000 had been launched to great acclaim the previous year, a beautiful vehicle that took design cues from the Jaguar E-type, and through its 2-litre engine had a top speed in excess of 140mph.

For the film, the car was equipped with an unique communication console developed by Sony. This included a miniature closed circuit colour TV, a two-way radio, hi-fi receiver and all contained within a voice controlled compartment. A miniature Sony video-tape unit was installed in the glove compartment and this could record from cameras concealed at the front and rear of the car.

Because filming had to stop at Himeji Castle, the 400 year-old gardens of the New Otani were used as a substitute for the ninja training ground. Here we see Bond practising with the ninja in the altogether lusher grounds than the rather summer-parched grass seen at the castle. The garden also doubled as Henderson's garden, combined with footage shot earlier in Shigetomiso. The exterior of Henderson's house where she and Bond pull up outside in the Toyota was said by Akiko Wakabayashi to be in Happo-en Shiroganedai, an area to the south of Tokyo's centre. Another and much more likely possibility comes from Kawashima Ichigai, the Japanese location manager is the inn or restaurant 大森の料亭「福久良」Fukuhisa Ryokan (with various spellings such as Fukukura) in the 1 Chome-8 Ōmorihonchō

The Definitive Story Of You Only Live Twice

area near Haneda. (Incidently two doubles are in the car when it pulls into the driveway; and the filming took place on the evening of 13 September.)

On 3 September, Connery visited one of the real ninja headquarters - well in truth not a ninja school but a karate school as some of the extras came from the Kyokushinkaikan Honbu Dojo.

Also worth noting before moving on to the next location that although the New Otani was used as the HQ of the Osato Chemical Engineering Co. Ltd, the address of the company was given as Marunouchi 2-58, Chiyoda-ku, Tokyo; and with the telephone number 211 3111. This area in Tokyo is known as being the commercial and financial district. Although the actual address does not exist, the building would be close to where today's Mitsubishi offices sit.

Then on 5, 6, and 7 September they filmed the sumo wrestling scene at Tokyo's sumo hall (known as the Kuramae Kokugikan, Kuramae 2 - chome 1-1, Taito-ku, Tokyo. This was the original building, which later was demolished and replaced by a more up-to-date facility.)

To enter the arena, Bond walks off the street into a beauty parlour.

In the scenes that follow, we see three leading *sumo* wrestlers: Sadanoyama Shinmatsu in the changing room and then a bout between Kotozakura Masakatsu and Fujinishiki Takemitsu as Bond meets Aki for the first time. The bout sequence was not filmed during a real tournament and the hall had been filled with spectators by advertising that a Bond movie was being shot. Among the spectators is the film director David Lean, who was visiting Tokyo following the success of *Doctor Zhivago.*

The newly built Nakano-shimbashi Station is featured in two scenes: Tiger's private train starts from here, and earlier Bond chases Aki down on to a platform from the single entrance at street level.

Graham Thomas

At one point Ken Adam recounted that he and Connery decided to try a Tokyo bathhouse. Ken said that the baths were mixed and the two were quite nervous about going naked into them. Although a lovely anecdote this may not be true as the baths in Tokyo were not mixed and Connery would have caused a riot if he had been seen naked in a public bath. More likely Ken was remembering the two of them visiting an *onsen* in one of the *ryokan* or hotels where they had stayed.

Several scenes feature Bond walking through the side streets of Ginza tracked by Aki. These are a combination of second unit photography and night shots of Connery walking through the West 5th Street area of the Ginza first on Ginza Suzuran Street where the rickshaw sequence takes place at the top of the street, the Mitake Button shop and Washington Shoes can be seen, before he cuts through a building. This alley is now between a shop called Mariage Frerez and a kimono store that is probably the one that can just been seen in the film. He then emerges a street away and into a narrow alley with Bar Lupin (B1F, 5-5-11 Ginza, Chuo-ku.) Here he opens a door with a sign saying Beauty Salon into the sumo ring, which of course is not there!

While filming, the cast took refuge in a jewellery shop called Miwa on〒104-0061 東京都中央区銀座6丁目7 - 2 in Ginza. The shop can be seen reflected on an opposite window in one of the cuts, and Connery was more than happy to sign an autograph.

The large sign in the film of Ginza 5th Street, which was opposite Miwa and where Bond and Aki drive off was taken down in the early 2000s.

(It is worth noting that all the shops have been rebuilt and hence the streets today do not look like anything in the films.)

The scenes of Bond and Aki driving through Ginza are a combination of the second unit using doubles, and blue screen set-ups back at Pinewood. We also see all the bright neon of Harumi-dori, Ginza in its full glory - for most Western audiences the sheer dazzle of colour would be mind-blowing. The tubular San-ai building can be seen and the neon included advertising for CBS, Furuya, Mitsubishi, Asahi Breweries, Toshiba, National televisions, and Snow White Shirayuki sake.

Later, the ubiquitous car chase scene races and swerves through the streets of Tokyo. We see several unidentifiable side streets but most likely in the Aoyoma, Shibuya-ku Higashi 3 and 4 chome areas, and then the Komazawa Olympic Park flashes past as does Yoyogi National Gymnasium. However two stand-ins are used in the live action, and again all close-ups use the blue-screen set-up in Pinewood where Bond and Aki are sitting in a mocked-up car.

Roald Dahl later said, 'I can remember Tokyo. When we were shooting some of those later sequences, and they needed another scene or a rewrite. I met with Lewis down in the bar in the Hilton Hotel and gave them something like 20 pages. He literally flipped through them and then said, 'That's fine.''

He and the first unit then returned to London on 19 September, to continue filming interiors at Pinewood's E-stage, and to start post-synching the dialogue.

The second unit remained in Tokyo to shoot more pick-up shots while a separate and specialist aerial unit filmed back in Kirishima using Kagoshima Airport as their base.

Kirishima

Behind Kagoshima lies the bleak and volcanic region of Ebino in the Kirishima National Park. On 18 September the aerial unit started filming the sequence where first Bond tests out Little Nellie and then starts to search for Blofeld's hideaway - offering the chance for some spectacular footage over the coastline and around the volcanoes. The next sequence has Bond pursued by four SPECTRE Bell-47 helicopters and the dogfight begins.

Little Nellie was flown not by Connery but by its builder Wing

Commander Ken Wallis, with filming usually starting at 6.00am in the morning and at a height of 6,000 feet. In total, Wallis made over sixty flights for the film and spent forty-six hours in the air.

Much was filmed around Mount Shinmoe but one sequence where Bond discovers that he is being pursued as he sees shadows on the mountainside was filmed at Sakarajima, an active volcano.

On the morning of 27 September, an accident occurred while filming the dog-fight: two helicopters collided and John Jordan, the cameraman, had his foot badly damaged and eventually it had to be amputated - though fortunately this did not stop him working in the future. Filming was stopped and further sequences of rockets firing and explosions exploding were shot in Torremolinos, Spain, and close-ups with Connery back in England.

Tokyo Bay

The final sequences shot in Japan were filmed at the end of September and into October and included a Boeing Vertol V-107 helicopter plucking up the villain's car with a giant magnet, filmed at the Mount Fuji International Speedway. Due to the helicopter then being damaged in a typhoon, it was another several weeks before the car was unceremoniously dumped into Tokyo Bay. However despite a rumour that it was allowed to sink into the sea, divers in fact recovered it.

Pinewood and Post Production

Back in England, filming on the giant volcano set started later than planned at the end of October. The set was, according to *The Times*, 126 feet high, and used 700 tons of structural steel, which was more than was used to build the Hilton Hotel (according that is to the BBC who also said that 8000 railways sleepers were used to create the platform, and enough canvas to make 4000 Boy Scout tents.) The total build cost was £350,000, and the structure could be seen three miles away from the A40 road to London.

One story has it that as it was being completed, Ken Adam asked Stanley Kubrick how to light it as it was so big. Kubrick was happy to give an opinion but arrived in the middle of the night so as not to be seen.

In the middle of November, the scenes with the light aircraft ferrying Bond to his supposed death were shot over a very English looking, Buckinghamshire/Oxfordshire countryside whereas this was supposed to be Japan; and the aircraft crashed landed at the disused Finmere aerodrome.

Principle photography did not finish until the middle of December, and then the production team had to shoot the model footage of the rockets in space, and the spaceman drifting to his death. This started in the first week of January and in the end post production was not completed until March 1967.

During this latter period, Maurice Binder's worked on his title sequence, which begins with the most dramatic shots of flowing larva, his trademark semi-naked girls, and a haunting song sung by Nancy Sinatra (albeit a combination of 25 different takes). The titles' backdrop of exploding volcanoes and flowing larva, used footage taken from the French documentary *Les rendezvous du diaboles.* This stunning film had been released in 1959, filmed by the geologist Haroun Tazief across many volcanic countries including Japan. He had been able to get dangerously close to the action, and the film amazed audiences and professional alike.

John Barry surpasses himself when it comes to composing the theme tune and the score captures and combines a mysterious sense of the Orient. Fellow Oscar-winner Leslie Bricusse, whose father Cedric had worked at Kemsley Newspapers, penned the lyrics. This of course is where Fleming worked but whether the two really knew each other is open to debate, as it would appear that his job was supervising the loading of newspapers on to the vans every night.

Bricusse wrote the words while visiting the Hollywood star Kirk Douglas in Palm Springs:

You only live twice or so it seems

One life for yourself and one for your dreams

You drift through the years and life seems tame

Till one dream appears and love is it's name.

Altogether this provides one of the most beautiful, erotic and strangely poignant openings of the Bond series. Of course, with all Bond films there is also the alternative version, in this instance, the singer Julie Rogers had recorded a different song for the title track but this was dropped and the producers asked for a revised song and a new singer. Sinatra was taken on.

Barry recorded his score at the London Bayswater studios of CTS, using an orchestra that was called the London Philharmonic but in reality not a fulltime orchestra but session musicians, many of whom had played with Barry previously.

Across the soundtrack itself, Barry creates a strong theme that is interwoven with many forms and Bond motifs whether hard and driving, action, love, or just to signify that this is the beauty of Japan. He later remarked that he was trying to entwine the elegance of Japan into the soundscape that he was creating.

Whicker's 53 minute documentary was first broadcast on primetime BBC2 on 25 March 1967. *The Times*' critic said it 'provided a splendid opportunity for the dry irony of Whicker' as he documented the fabulous locations in Japan and rubbed shoulders with the delectable Bond girls.

Less than three months later, with a running time of 116 minutes and an 'A' Certificate, *You Only Live Twice* was premiered in London with Her Majesty the Queen in the audience.

THE FILM

Prior to the launch of the film, the producers put a huge marketing campaign in motion, as they thought that this was going to be the last time that they would be able to use the power of Sean Connery. The posters were designed by two celebrated American designers Frank McCarthy and Robert McGinnis who had also worked on *Thunderball*. Much PR was undertaken with the media including special promotions with magazines such as *Car, Photoplay, Showtime, Blackbelt, Esquire* and even *Popular Science* and, of course, a swathe of merchandising deals were negotiated including Antler 007 suitcases in two sizes with the larger size selling for £17 7s; a special Scaletrix kit for £11 9s 2d; *You Only Live Twice* bubble gum; an Airfix 1:24 model of the Toyota car and Little Nellie, and even 007 underwear made by Morley. Other items included sets of fan cards, which were described thus: 'United Artists Exploitation Department has produced these special fan cards for mass distribution in swimming pools, dance halls, coffee bars, record and music shops.'

In the UK they cost 35 shillings for 1000 and could be overprinted with the local cinema details. 'Flood the town with this seat-selling accessory' distributors were urged.

A tie-in was arranged with Pan American to promote flights to Japan. Selfridges in London mounted a large window display that included props from the film.

Graham Thomas

In the UK and US, the cinema exhibitors received a campaign pack laying out the PR programme and the material they could order. This was extensive and indicated the optimism of the producers about the films box office appeal. They included for use in local newspapers, a Bond crossword, a spot-the-difference competition, and a competition where readers would have to select eight photos of the Bond girls in their order of preference. The exhibitor would have to pay for the printing block but they were told it would have to be provided to their local newspaper for free. Photographic enlargements for front-of-house displays were available or they could be used for any promotional stunts. However, the promoters were reminded that they did not own the material, that they could use it only under licence, and it could not be sold on.

Distributors were also reminded that as much of the film was set in Japan, they could create their own promotions using Japanese products as prizes including cameras, transistor radios, and tape recorders.

It was announced that there would be a 'mammoth' nationwide promotional campaign tied in with the launch of the Pan paperback and 'an exciting range of cut-out showcard units' were available for display in bookstores.

In the US, a radio campaign was mounted (the UK was yet to enjoy commercial radio), and also a one hour, colour TV programme was broadcast called *Welcome to Japan, Mr Bond*. This was first shown on 2 June on NBC in the timeslot usually reserved for *The Man From Uncle*. The documentary starred Lois Maxwell and Desmond Llewelyn as Miss Moneypenny and Q, with Kate O'Mara as Moneypenny's unnamed assistant. Through the use of clips, they talk about Bond's adventures in *Dr. No*, *From Russia with Love*, *Goldfinger* and *Thunderball* and, as a way of introducing the new film, they speculate on Bond's latest assignments, and show clips from *You Only Live Twice*.

And to introduce some modicum of suspense, a storyline is

teased out about a woman (who is never directly shown) who is determined to be Bond's new lover. She is seen holding a Pan paperback copy of *On Her Majesty's Secret Service*, which suggests that the producers had finally decided that this should be the next film. (Although it would be another year before cameras turned over.)

At least one promotional booklet was produced in Japan by the publisher Visier with stills and stories from the film, while *Screen*, a Japanese monthly magazine, had already published a *You Only Live Twice* special edition with 156 pages, and 200 photographs taken while the film was being shot on location. In fact it has been issued in October before the film was even finished and had featured spreads from Kagoshima, Akime, Kirishima, Kobe, Himeji, Nachi, and Tokyo. Five pages were colour with the others printed in black and white. Behind this idea were Toho, who decided without telling the UK producers, that they would create some positive publicity to counter the largely negative stories that had been circulating.

The sheet music of the title song was published, with the copyright owned by United Artists Music and not by Barry, and the sole selling agents noted as Campbell, Connelly and Co of 10 Denmark Street in London – otherwise known as Tin Pan Alley.

One of the two Toyota cars was shipped to Europe and exhibited at the 1967 Paris, Brussels, Amsterdam and Geneva Motor Shows. It was estimated it was admired by over 50,000 people.

The London premiere was held on 12 June 1967, a royal premiere at the Odeon Leicester Square, sponsored by the Variety Club of Great Britain in aid of the YMCA, and Imperial Cancer Research Fund. Sean Connery by now was sporting a moustache and had discarded his toupee. Afterwards the Queen wearing a glittering tiara was presented to Connery, Gilbert, and the producers, and other celebrities such as Laurence Harvey, Dick van Dyke, and Phil Silvers. None of the Japanese actors attended.

The following night a second special charity midnight matinee took place in aid of the Arthritis and Rheumatism Council. Also on 13 June, the film went on general release in the UK, and opened in New York at the Astor, the Victoria, the Baronet and Loew's Orpheum with a huge billboard dominating Time Square.

While the public enjoyed it, many of the critics were less enthusiastic. This was the first Bond film to feature significant amounts of gadgetry, which was said to be gimmicky, and also the whole hijacking of rockets was felt to be preposterous and far-fetched. Another valid criticism was that it did not give enough screen time to Blofeld (and his rather terrified cat that was always trying to escape out of shot). And the two Japanese girls did not make for great Bond girls as they said so little - not surprisingly as they could barely speak English and although Mie Hama was always going to be dubbed, it was thought getting them to say little in the first instance was best. Other bizarre plot lines included having Bond fake his death and enter Japan secretly (in earlier films he was quite happy to enter a country on a commercial flight) for no discernible purpose other than that the 'enemy' would take less notice of him. (That he soon thereafter visits the enemy's offices is another matter.)

Malcolm Muggeridge, another former intelligence officer, and who also didn't like the novel as was noted earlier, wrote, '*You Only Live Twice* has a decidedly perfunctory air...'

The US critics found the script's *double entendres* heavy going and the infamous Pauline Kael wrote that the style had been coarsened and the screenplay 'gaggy.'

Contrary to the trend, *The Times* critic judged the film to be a return to form and that the gadgetry was used well to further the plot. Indeed there is much to admire: Barry's music is superlative, the action sequences are generally done well (the fight at Kobe is superb), and the spectacular locations draw it all together. On the downside, it seems clear that Connery was not at his happiest and rather than moving like a cat, the trait that first attracted him to Broccoli, he seems to slouch his way through the film, Gilbert's direction is erratic at times, and Freddie Young's cinematographic skills are largely wasted. (The most interesting shots are either second unit or the aerial photography.) On top of this, are the any number of continuity mistakes that suggest either a rather tardy attitude or just incompetence – though such lapses were not unique to *You Only Live Twice*, as *Thunderball*, for example, had even more.

The Japanese premiere took place a few days later on 17 June, with Connery absent. The literal Japanese translation was *007 Dies Twice*, in Japanese 007は二度死ぬ.

Inevitably with Bondo-mania still sweeping Japan, the film garnered excited reviews and was seen to be a positive depiction of Japanese culture. The film had been blown up to 70mm and had a six track stereo track mixed on it (the UK film was released in mono.) It was subtitled - although when it was first shown on TBS TV in Japan in 1978 it was dubbed.

The *Japan Times* reported that despite the unfavourable publicity received during its filming in Japan, the crowds were huge at the beautiful art deco Hibiya Theatre when over 11,000 people saw the film in six showings on its first Saturday, and those who could not find seats were happy to stand.

(Bondo-mania had really taken off in Japan with the release of *Goldfinger*. This led to any number of spy-related TV programmes and local films as well as huge market in spy-related toys for children.)

Not surprisingly *You Only Live Twice* proved to be the most popular foreign film in Japan in 1967 - with *Grand Prix* coming a distant second, it too featuring a Japanese star Toshiro Mifune. The film's box-office success repeated that of *Thunderball* and a couple of years later *On Her Majesty's Secret Service* was equally popular. (In 1967, the most popular film in Japan was *Kurobe no Taiyo*, a story that showed the problems of constructing the Kurobe dam.)

Back in UK, the film moved to the London Pavilion cinema on Picaddilly Circus and for those who love triva the outside of the cinema, displaying the posters can be seen in the opening sequence the Russian film Мертвый сезон 1 серия. (Translated as Dead Season and a thriller.) The London Pavilion was sometimes used for Bond premieres but not with YOLT; it played here across September '67 which must be when the footage was shot.

The film's soundtrack had been released as an LP but over ensuing months while soundtracks such as *Doctor Zhivago* and *Fiddler on the Roof* were in the Top 20, *You Only Live Twice* did not trouble the UK charts, and Nancy Sinatra's single (a different recording from that heard in the film and one that had been rearranged in Hollywood) squeezed into the Top 20 for two weeks only - but that said, this was the best performing title track to date. Barry also released his own instrumental version but this failed to bother the charts. The single was also released in Japan and many other markets globally.

Meanwhile the original soundtrack LP released in the US had a slightly different set of tracks as it featured 'You Only Live Twice – End Title' with a vocal by Sinatra whereas the UK version had an instrumental version. The former was what was actually heard on the film and when the LP was reissued in the UK this vocal track was included.

In Japan, the soundtrack was released in a gatefold sleeve with the inner spread featuring images from the film and a summary of the plot.

Shortly after the film's release Mie Hama posed naked for the June issue of *Playboy* as part of the publicity for the film, with text provided by Dahl.

Other actresses who took small parts in the film also featured in the magazine including Hisako Katakura, Yuka Mimami and Kiyomi Kobayashi. Akiko Wakabayashi was also part of the photo-spread but clothed a little more discretely. *Playboy* helpfully pointed out that she was taller than the norm for a Japanese girl, and that her measurements were 35-23-35.5 inches.

Pan released a tie-in edition of the novel to coincide with the film's release. They had been the paperback publisher since *Casino Royale* appeared, and when the films were released they always published a new edition, starting with *Dr No* in 1962.

You Only Live Twice was no exception. Their initial edition of the novel was published in 1965 a year after the Cape hard cover, and had then gone to its second printing in 1966. For the release of the film in 1967, they designed a new cover that featured publicity shots from the film. As the book used some of the second printing sheets this has led some people to think it was published in 1966 but in fact it was published in early 1967, a couple of months before the launch of the film, and the use of the publicity shots was all part of the teaser marketing campaign.

My own final say, is that it remains one of my favourite Bond movies, highly watchable, and with much to enjoy.

Connery of course thought he was going to call it a day. In a final interview with the BBC when asked why, he said,

'I've had a long sort of innings as it were, very intense, and I want to change direction, take another breath and do something else.'

So this is your last Bond film?

'Yes. I'm very tired because it's like a long uphill drive.'

Looking back how do you feel about giving up the money and glamour, the whole fascade of Bond?

'Well I suppose when you are familiar with something you just accept it, and it comes to mean something else to somebody else. Whereas I'm ready in myself to make a change and go in a new direction.'

THE MAN WITH THE RED TATTOO

In the first edition of this book I focused purely on the connection between Japan and *You Only Live Twice*. However, I was asked by a number of people to include a chapter on the Japanese connection with *The Man With The Red Tattoo*, the follow-on novel by Raymond Benson. Initially I demurred as Benson himself has written about the background to the book and I was unsure what I could add. In addition, I had not visited all the locations featured within the plot.

I am still unsure but I was finally persuaded because an important part of *The Man With The Red Tattoo* takes place around an area of Japan that I have a lot of affection for, namely the Seto Inland Sea. Consequently this chapter gives me the opportunity to bring to a wider audience, one of the most unspoilt, beautiful and indeed interesting parts of Japan.

This is not the only part of Japan to feature in the book. Much action happens around Tokyo (such as the Imperial Hotel, the Ginza, and the Tsukiji fish market) and in the northern island of Hokkaido but these are all places that feature in guidebooks and many travel articles on Japan so I will only touch on those parts that I know well - although I find it fascinating how quickly descriptions date nowadays. For example, who would ever have thought that Tsukiji would relocate in 2018, for example, but then Japan is a country in a constant state of metamorphosis.

The Man with the Red Tattoo was first published in 2002 and the story opens with a girl falling ill while flying on a Japanese Airlines 747, one that does not boast flatbed seats in Business Class so passengers are seated in rows. 'Quelle horreur.' Just sixteen years later this is so out of date as to seem truly antiquated. (I wondered whether in another sixteen years time, today's flying experience will seem just as antiquated.)

2002 was a year when laptops were still called 'laptop computers.' This was a time before smartphones, and a Palm Pilot was Bond's choice of handset.

The book retains some connection to *You Only Live Twice* as Tiger Tanaka remains a central character but is now a semi-retired official within the *Koan-Chosa-Cho;* and before M sends Bond to Japan he is apprehensive because of the memories it might dredge up about experiences he would rather forget.

Of course the novel has to overcome the passage of time. Almost forty years separate the two books but Bond is still going strong both physically and with his relationship to women, while Tiger is slipping into retirement.

Never mind.

Back to the book.

Bond flies to Tokyo's Narita Airport on a JAL flight. Narita had only been built as the new international airport after the visits by Fleming, Bond and Connery. They had flown into Haneda but after the construction of Narita, Haneda was used purely for domestic flights. This has now changed again and Haneda now accepts international flights (and BA, for example, fly in with a morning flight assigned the number BA007).

After arriving, Bond's adventures unfold across a string of locations throughout Japan but the climax of the story is the villain's attempt to assassinate world leaders while they are in Japan for a G8 Summit. The exceedingly clever *modus operandi* is to use genetically modified mosquitos who, after biting into human flesh, leave behind a fatal virus that has no cure.

The Summit takes place on the island of Naoshima (a G8 summit had actually taken place in Japan in 2000 but in Okinawa). In a blog, Benson notes that when writing the novel he would undertake research by traveling to the locations where Bond's adventures would take place...'the most significant place we visited was the island of Naoshima, located in the Inland Sea in Kagawa Prefecture.'

To reach the island a ferry needs to be boarded. Bond had flown from Tokyo to the city of Okayama and then had taken a car to Uno, a small sleepy port where he caught a ferry. At one time, before the building of the three bridges in the 1980s-90s that now link Honshu and Shikoku, this was the main port to undertake that journey. Now it only serves islands in the Inland Sea and so is considerably quieter.

Referring back to Fleming's own journey when he traveled with Saito-san and Hughes through the Inland Sea in the early 1960s: Saito-san muses on his dream to open a hotel on one of the islands in the Inland Sea. That dream went unrealised but Naoshima boasts one of the world's most splendid hotels, one that only has a dozen rooms and is integrated into Benesse House, one of the world's most stunning art museums, and one designed by the revered Japanese architect Tadao Ando. It is here that the G8 summit will take place.

Benson mentions that Benesse can be found close to the Seto Ohashi Bridge and rightly describes it as extraordinary structure.

But a word about Benesse House and the hotel.

Naoshima is known as the art island not just because of the museum but because the island is studded with *in situ* art installations that can be found out in the open and within 'art houses' - reclaimed village homes that would otherwise have long sunk into the ground.

Benesse Art Site Naoshima came about because of the vision of two men: Tetsuhiko Fukutake, the president of Fukutake Publishing had a dream to create a meeting place in the Seto Inland Sea where children from all over the world would gather; Chikatsugu Miyake, then mayor of Naoshima, dreamt of creating a cultural and educational area on the island.

They met in 1985 and began to hatch a plan that would make their dreams a reality. This started with a camp where people slept in yurts, and then in 1992 the Benesse House museum was opened with artworks by some of the world's foremost contemporary artists. Over the years, the number of art works within the museum but also outside the building has grown exponentially and the island is now recognised as one of the greatest, most distinctive museums in the world.

Benson's description of the museum is still largely true today: 'a magnificent modern building made of marble, concrete and steel' and I would add glass, creating a structure that flows along ramps and stairs and across a multitude of open levels.

Bruce Nauman's neon sculpture, '100 Live and Die' is the central piece on entering the museum. Other works are by Warhol, Haring, Johns, Twombly, Long and more - many of them being site specific.

Some artworks described by Benson are no longer exhibited: William Kanas' 'Love Hurts' a large sculptured heart pieced by an arrow was part of a temporary exhibition of work by YBAs - Young British Artists. No such artist exists. In fact no YBA temporary exhibition was held at the museum and this was a plot device within the novel.

In 1995, the Benesse House Oval was opened as an exclusive hotel perched high on a hill over-looking the museum and the

The Definitive Story Of You Only Live Twice

Seto Inland Sea. The Oval has a large flat fountain pool in its centre surrounded by the guest rooms. The water reflects the sky and provides a constant backdrop of trickling water to soothe the soul. Floor-to-ceiling windows in the rooms proffer panoramic views of the Inland Sea and yet the Oval also appears to be set within the summit of the hill.

Bond is met by Tiger and is taken to the hotel by a monorail that winds round a steep hill. Not a great distance and the journey takes about 5 minutes.

Bond's mission is to protect the British Prime Minister. He wears an Ozwald Boateng suit, the designer being very much *outre dig* at the turn of the century, and someone who I had dinner with in Tokyo at the time. Underneath this Bond wore a rig that would protect him from mosquito bites.

Do the deadly mosquitos escape?

Do they attack?

Is the Prime Minister killed?

Well I won't give the ending away and instead will finish off the chapter by briefly reviewing the other Japanese locations in the novel.

Rather than taking a BA flight, Bond flew with JAL from London. In fact in the first years of the 21 Century he could have also chosen a Virgin Atlantic flight - since discontinued - and then as now ANA also fly direct. Obviously the travel policy at HQ did not require operatives to fly the flag but then Bond was partial to Japanese girls and thought that the JAL hostesses (today we would say cabin crew) epitomised all that he admired about Japanese women.

This time Bond ate a Japanese dinner accompanied by *Ginjo sake*. This is not a brand name but a description of a type of *sake* where some 40 per cent of the outer rice husk has been milled away. The greater the percentage removed, the more delicate the end result. Usually if the *sake* is labeled *Ginjo*, it means distilled alcohol has been added; if labeled *Junmai Ginjo*, it means no additional alcohol has been added. Even if *Ginjo* it is still premium *sake* and should be definitely served chilled.

Once in the centre of Tokyo it is good to see that Bond was shown Hachiko the dog at Shibuya Station. This was before the Richard Gere film made the dog internationally famous. Here Bond got out of the car as he is meeting Tiger. As he looked around he observed how young everyone was! I assume that this was an indication of Bond ageing. At the time, Shibuya still had a few *gangaru* girls hanging around although they were now a little passé. But Bond did notice the *gyaru* girls - still a feature of Tokyo. These are the High School girls who hitch up their usually knee-length school skirts to become micro-skirts and wear loose socks that fall about their ankle. Too young again, he thought.

Besides being a place renowned as a gathering point for the young and fashionable, Shibuya has its ubiquitous crossing, the one always seen in films and documentaries about Tokyo, the one where thousands of people stream from different directions across an intersection.

Close by is Meji Jinju Shrine, which Bond and Tiger visit. This perhaps mirrors the visit to the Ise Shrine in *You Only Live Twice*.

Are there caves under Tokyo, as Tiger has the use of Government Residence in a cave under Yoyogi Park. Unknown to me but then they are secret. Here they sip *sake*, and this time Tiger offers both cold and warm, and Bond leaves it to him to make a decision - warm was brought in.

Shinjuku was described by Benson as place that surpasses Times Square, Piccadilly, the Sunset Strip and Las Vegas. True. Specifically Bond and Tiger were going to the seediest bit of all. Kabukicho where the yakuza hang-out in their darkened Mercedes, and where sex in all its manifestations is on sale. A warren of streets and alleys and where some very good bars can be found and, of course, it is a soapland, where the process of cleansing the body is possibly the most thrilling that is possible. A step up from when Fleming visited a bath house.

Nonetheless Bond had time for a bowl of *udon*, a type of wheat noodle made thickly and while served in a variety of ways is often served with either a hot or cold broth.

Bond stayed at the Imperial Hotel, where Fleming had met Somerset Maugham for lunch. He enjoyed it because of its history and because it was one of the first hotels to serve pork and beef in its restaurant. Of course this was a different hotel than the one where Fleming had lunched: that hotel designed by Frank Lloyd Wright had been demolished and replaced in the 1970s by a rather boring slab of architecture, with further wings added in the 1980s.

Another hotel that Bond visits is the Takanawa Prince Hotel in Shinagawa where Tiger had a satellite office. From here, Bond could see Tokyo Tower.

Bond also has a chase around the Tsuji Market and then the *kabuki* theatre in the Ginza. He also ate a second bowl of *udon* - a good choice.

Sapporo is where the HQ of one of the yakuza front organisations could be found. To reach there Bond caught the overnight Casiopeia, a luxury train. Japan has a number of these that ply different routes around the country. It was noted of course that the train left on time. On the way, the action ratchets up in the Seikan Tunnel.

However he did not get on with *natto,* which was described as a putrid concoction that made him gag. It is a fermented dish that defeats many foreigners.

The Kuril Islands to the north of Hokkaido were once Japanese territory but at the end of the Second World War were annexed by the Russians who subsequently have refused to hand them back. The arguments as in any territorial dispute are complex and in part it is because no final or permanent peace treaty was signed between the two nations and while they are not at war, neither are they at peace in the strict sense of the word. One of the islands, Etorofu, was where the yakuza organisation had their operations but as access to Etorofu is limited and travel there not easy it is not worth dwelling on the place. After all, it is just trees and bears.

This finally brings us to the end of the story.

POSTSCRIPT

When Connery flew to Japan he was living in Acton but shortly after the premiere of *You Only Live Twice* he put the house on the market for £17,950. A week after this sale was announced, one of Fleming's former homes, the one near Canterbury was also put on the market for £26,000.

Fleming had now been dead for several years but the films were growing in popularity. The novels though while not out of fashion were becoming dated. In 1963, when Fleming was finishing off *You Only Live Twice* John Le Carre had transformed the genre when he published *The Spy Who Came In From The Cold*. Here was a story where the spy's world was a huge distance from Bond: no glamour and no gadgets just a rather mucky and murky world of dubious values, and mistakes. It was said to be authentic and cynical. Len Deighton was also writing in a similar mold, and had already published *The Ipcress File*. Would Fleming have changed his approach? Or would he have killed Bond off?

Taking advantage of his brother's success, in 1967 Neil Connery starred in the Italian spy comedy *O.K. Connery*. The cast included several actors from *You Only Live Twice*: Bernard Lee, Lois Maxwell, and Yasuko Yama who had appeared as one of the bath girls under the name Yee-Wah Yang. In fact this was her original name as she was Hong Kong born but her family had moved to England. She was only a part-time actress but and had appeared in an episode of *Emergency Ward 10* in the UK. However, after *O.K. Connery* she disappeared from the movie industry.

The official follow-up film was *On Her Majesty's Secret Service* with George Lazenby taking over the role, with Connery subsequently reappearing for the last time in *Diamonds Are Forever*. (Other than the lamentable *Never Say Never*, which was not part of the franchise.)

In 1990 a marble monument was erected on a hill overlooking Akime harbour, and engraved with the James Bond logo and the words 'Our James Bond film, You Only Live Twice was filmed on location here at Akime.' Underneath this inscription are the engraved signatures of Albert R. Broccoli, Sean Connery and Tetsuro Tamba.

Dikko Henderson or rather Richard Hughes died in January 1984 when still living in Hong Kong. He had submitted his column for the *Far Eastern Economic Review* in December 1983, which proved to be his last. Of course he had continued to preside over Alcoholics Synonymous right up until his death. Indeed, as a lapsed Catholic, he did not take a last supper but a last luncheon: this at a Christmas gathering of the Alcoholics in the FCC where he drank his usual tipple of Russian vodka before lunch, followed by wine. A few days later he was taken to hospital where he died.

Jack Condor, the Hong Kong *bon vivant* and tavern manager had died before Hughes in Friday 18 June 1976 After a service at the Union Church Kennedy, Hughes and the other mourners followed the cortege to Cape Collinson crematorium.

Of the two Bond girls? Akiko Wakabayashi, made one more film, and then a final appearance in a TV series in 1971. She then all but disappeared as she had suffered a number of injuries while acting and these became increasingly painful and debilitating. She resurfaced in 2006, when interviewed by the fanzine *G-Fan*. In this very rare interview, she said, 'James Bond in the movie is a ladies' man, but Sean-san is a warm-hearted honest man. He has a clear vision as an actor. He can be stubborn from time to time, but he is a real man with a bit of old-fashioned taste.'

Mie Hama never appeared in another foreign production but she starred in a further seventeen films in Japan until she brought her film career to a halt in 1975 and moved into television. Since then she has remained a celebrity in her home country becoming a television and radio host, a spokesperson for the need to preserve old farms and farming techniques, a lover of folk art, and the author of 14 books on topics such as child-rearing, manners and self-discovery. She also made an appearance in the 1989 film *Kitchen*. When *You Only Live Twice* celebrated its 50 anniversary in 2017, she gave an interview to the *New York Times*, when she said that after filming she did not meet Sean Connery again but, like Wakabayashi, commented on how she admired Connery and how kind he had been. Her latest book is called *Solitude Can Be a Wonderful Thing*.

Neither of the two Bond girls maintained close contact with each other after the film's release and the publicity campaign had finished. The Hibiya Theatre, where the film premiered in Tokyo closed and was demolished in 1984.

Donald Pleasance died in 1995 and Tetsurō Tamba in 2006. The latter had been a prolific actor up until his death appearing in both Japanese films and TV dramas but only one further western film according to the online database Imdb. Karin Dor, the flamed haired villainess died in 2017. She of course, no matter what else she played, was forever known as a Bond girl just as Shinmoedake when it erupts (as it did in 2018 for example) is now always referenced in international news as the James Bond volcano.

Lewis Gilbert died in Monaco on 23 February 2018, at the age of 97.

Roald Dahl was not asked to write another Bond script and he once said he was disappointed by this as he thought he'd 'done a good job, and it was done out of nothing.'

Japan failed to feature again in either films or novels until the publishing in 2002 of Benson's follow-on novel *The Man with the Red Tattoo*.

Then out of the blue Hashima, an island off Nagasaki and often known as Battleship Island because of its silhouette, acted as the inspiration for Raoul Silva's lair - the rather nasty villain played by Javier Bardem in *Skyfall* released in 2012. Inspiration because none of the sequences were filmed *in situ* but rather back at Pinewood, and in the film the island is identified as being close to Macau and not a Japanese island at all.

Hong Kong, a city that Fleming much admired, had not featured in any of the novels although if he had lived longer perhaps he would have used it as a setting in a later book - unless he had killed Bond off. However, in the films it was to appear in *The Man With the Golden Gun,* and briefly in *Die Another Day*.

Trains have featured heavily in both novels and films, and in 2018, the Romancecar trains that Fleming had so much enjoyed and admired on his first trip were still running, albeit with updated stock. However one model made its final trip that year, and while this was introduced in 1980 it was close in design to the original. Consequently, a set of stamps were issued to commemorate its passing, and that of an era.

The much lamented demolishment of the original wing of Hotel Okura where Bond stayed was covered in the chapter on the hotel. Fortunately, the iconic lobby lounge is to be recreated in what will be called the Prestige Tower, scheduled to open in 2019.

On 21 February 2019 the industry publication *Production Weekly* included a listing in its newsletter for "Bond 25 w/t Shatterhand", with shooting due to start at Pinewood Studios on 6 April, 2019, and the film scheduled for release in 2020. This created quite a stir in the media. Was the film going to be called Shatterhand everyone speculated?

The film's director is Cary Joji Fukunaga, an American with a Japanese father. Whether he is playing on his heritage to create the working title and whether the working title and the film has anything to do with Japan, we will have to wait and see. (After all the w/t of a film may not be used ultimately, and they are a good ruse to create rumour and social media chat.)

Yet. In fact Fukunaga did not chose the working title. In a *Production Weekly* listing from August 2018 - and before he was appointed to the role - the Shatterhand w/t had already been noted but for some reason received little media attention - other than a few rumours did circulate that the new film will draw on *You Only Live Twice*.

In writing this book, I came to realise that the Bond connections with Japan are more numerous and deeper than I had thought at the outset of my quest and, of course, he is just as popular today in the country as he ever was. But is that a good thing? Perhaps the last word should go to the poet and author James Kirkup, who's books had become a reference for Fleming. In 1970, Kirkup wrote in *Japan Behind The Fan*,

'Today I find appalling Japan's lack of common public morality, her increasing materialism and heedless search for immediate satisfactions, her totally uncritical absorption of many of the worst features of American and European life, her inane crazes for motoring, American musicals, golf, bowling, James Bond and American English conversation lessons.'

THE AUTHOR

The author lives sometimes in Japan, and sometimes in the UK.

@japanauthor

grahamthomas.wordpress.com

BIBLIOGRAPHY

The author gratefully acknowledges the following as selected sources and help when taking this journey across Japan:

You Only Live Twice. Ian Fleming. Jonathan Cape, 1964.

Australian Dictionary of Biography. On-line

Thrilling Cities. Ian Fleming. Jonathan Cape, 1963.

Foreign Devil, Thirty Years of Reporting from the Far East. Richard Hughes. Andre Deutsch, 1972.

These Horned Islands. James Kirkup. Collins, 1962.

The Man with the Golden Typewriter. Ian Fleming's James Bond Letters. Fergus Fleming. Bloomsbury. 2015.

Some Kind of Hero: The Remarkable Story of the James Bond Films. Matthew Field, Ajay Chowdhury. The History Press. 2015

The James Bond Archives. Paul Duncan. Taschen 2015.

Bond and Beyond. Tom Sotor, Image Pub of New York. 1993.

The Life of Ian Fleming. John Pearson. Jonathan Cape Ltd., 1966.

Ian Fleming. Andrew Lyce. Orion. 1995.

This is Japan, Edited by Torao Saito. Asahi Shimbun. 1961, 1964, and other editions.

Company Confessions, Christopher Moran, Biteback Publishing, 2015.

Storyteller: The Authorised Biography of Roald Dahl. Donald Sturrock. William Collins. 2016.

Roald Dahl's love-hate relationship with Hollywood, Daily Telegraph, 22 July 2016.

Welcome to Pinewood Studios Mr Bond. Classic Bond 24 September 2017.

Roald Dahl: A Biography, Jeremy Treglown. Harvest/HBJ Book. Published 1995.

Facsimile Hong Kong Standard. Produced in 2017 by Robert Gritten.

G-Fan 2006, Vol 1 Issue. 76, pg. 8-11. Armand Vaquer and Brett Homenick, "Akiko Wakabayashi, An Exclusive G-FAN Interview"

Starlog Magazine, Issue 169, August 1991. He Only Lived Twice, Dahl interview in 1980 by Tom Sotor. Available online.

Various archived editions of The Times.

The Japanese "drink of the Gods": economic and managerial challenges of sake production in the recent decades Tatiana Bouzdine-Chameeva and Mari Ninomiya. Refereed paper – 5th International Academy of Wine Business Research Conference, 8-10 Feb. 2010 Auckland (NZ)

The History of Mitsubishi Corporation in London: 1915 to Present Day by Pernille Rudlin. Routledge.

Japan Times, Sunday, June 18, 1967

007 James Bond, A Report. O F Snelling, Neville Spearman Limited, 1964.

Britain and Japan: Biographical Portraits, Volume VI Global Oriental. Cortazzi, Hugh [Compiled and Edited by] Ian Fleming chapter by, John Hatcher.

The Tatler. 17 January, 1962.

Photoplay. August, 1966.

Japan's fleet of Flying Fortress. Robert C Mikesh, Aviation History July 2010, Vol.20.

Origins Of Irish Free Masonry In Hong Kong. D Roy Murray. Reprinted CANMAS, November, 2005.

Japan Experiences - Fifty Years, One Hundred Views: Post-War Japan Through British Eyes. Hugh Cortazzi. Japan Society. 2001